Bizarre
CATS

Brad Steiger is the author of more than a hundred books with over fifteen million copies in print, ranging from biographies to the inspirational to the phenomenal. He lives with his wife in Iowa.

Brad Steiger is also the author of *Bizarre Crime*, published by Pan Books.

BRAD STEIGER

PAN BOOKS
LONDON, SYDNEY AND AUCKLAND

First published 1993 by Pan Books Ltd

a division of Pan Macmillan Publishers Limited
Cavaye Place London SW10 9PG
and Basingstoke

Associated companies throughout the world

ISBN 0 330 33036 5

1 3 5 7 9 8 6 4 2

A CIP catalogue record for this book is available from
the British Library

Typeset by Cambridge Composing (UK) Limited, Cambridge
Printed and bound in Great Britain by
Cox & Wyman Ltd, Reading, Berkshire

CONTENTS

CHAPTER FOUR: **THE TOUGH GUYS —
CATS WITH MORE THAN
NINE LIVES!**

CHAPTER FIVE: **MEAN AND SCARY CATS**

CONTENTS

CHAPTER SIX: **EERIE GHOST CATS**

CHAPTER SEVEN: **CATS WITH WEIRD TALENTS**

CHAPTER EIGHT: **FIND YOUR IDEAL CAT IN THE STARS**

CHAPTER ONE

FANTASTIC FELINE FACTS ABOUT OUR NUMBER ONE PET

RECORD-BREAKING CATS

Cats seem to be everywhere these days

The Cat Fanciers' Association now recognizes thirty-five different breeds of our feline friend. With an estimated 62.4 million of the furry creatures in the United States alone, their number has doubled in the last decade.

Cats are living longer

The average life expectancy of cats has nearly doubled since the 1930s – from eight years to sixteen.

The oldest living cat on record

Although a cat is not really considered a senior citizen until it has passed its tenth birthday, the longevity champ is 'Puss', who passed away in 1939, just one day after the thirty-sixth celebration of his natal anniversary.

Cats are prolific critters

The cat's prolific nature, together with improved health care, has certainly been a contributing factor to its great numbers in 1993. Mother cats have produced up to nineteen kittens per litter.

The largest recorded number of kittens born in a lifetime of fertility to a single female cat is 420.

And we do take good care of them

In an average year, cat owners in the United States alone spend $2.15 billion on cat food – and $295 million on cat litter.

Goodbye, Felix and Josephine

The names currently most popular for pet cats are Tiger and Samantha.

What a rough tongue you have, Samantha!

Those sandpaper kisses from your pet are due to numerous tiny knobs called *papillae* on the surface if kitty's tongue. They are shaped like backward hooks, and are designed to hold food and to provide the abrasiveness your cat needs for those endless hours of grooming.

A whole lot of sleeping going on

Yes, your cat does sleep a lot. Cats are, in fact, the sleepiest of all animals. If you added up all the minutes your pet spent in catnaps each day, the total would probably come to around sixteen hours.

If, however, for any reason your cat should be deprived of the amino acid tryptophan, which is found in milk, eggs and poultry, it would become a jittery insomniac in a very short time.

Your powers of observation have served you well: your cat does have more than one eyelid

It has three, as a matter of fact.

Cats can't really see in the dark

And a cat's daytime vision is only fair – but they can see better than their owners in semi-darkness.

Their eyes don't really shine in the dark, either. Cats' eyes contain highly reflective cells that collect light from even very dim sources. When you flash a light on a cat in the darkness, these reflective cells make it appear as if its eyes are glowing.

Although cats have long been considered colour-blind, recent tests indicate that they can distinguish between some basic colours paired together, such as red and blue.

But, boy, do they have good ears!

A cat's hearing rates as one of the sharpest in all the animal kingdom. If you have ever wondered why your cat is always waiting for you at the door, it's because it can hear your footsteps from hundreds of feet away.

THOSE DARNED MICE ARE SINGING OFF-KEY AGAIN!

It has long been noted that cats are supersensitive to discord and will soon vacate a room if there are off-key singers or musicians performing. On the other hand, cats genuinely appear to appreciate good music and harmony.

Biologists have studied a number of singing mice that exhibit two-octave ranges and tempos that vary between two and six notes per second. It is quite likely that all mice sing, producing songs that are similar to the chirping and twittering of small birds, but with a great deal more variety.

If you have not been aware of any rodent chorales blessing you with one of their concerts, it's probably because the vast majority of mice sing in pitches far too high for the human ear, perhaps very much like the supersonic squeaks of bats. The mice that you have heard may be compared to the basses and baritones of a human choral group, while most of their fellow warblers are high sopranos.

While there are undoubtedly a few humans who have the auditory sensitivity to eavesdrop on a night at the rodent opera, it may be assumed that cats, with their remarkable sense of hearing, present a captive audience to the pesky little squeakers.

Everyone knows that cats enjoy an occasional snack of

mouse meat, but some scientists have theorized that cats primarily pursue mice when the little rodents sing off-key and upset the feline insistence upon harmony.

A number of friends who are musicians and composers have credited some of their success to their critical cats' acceptance or rejection of their work. Imagine those unfortunate miniature madrigal singers receiving the ultimate negative criticism of their performance from a cat with a splitting headache!

THE WORLD CHAMPION MOUSE-CATCHER!

In the light of the fantastic feline fact detailed above, Towser, a tabby in charge of rodent control at a Scottish distillery, was either the world's champion mouse-catcher or the world's most sensitive music critic. At any rate, by the age of twenty-one, the records show that she had caught 23,000 mice.

Your cat does walk differently from your dog

The giraffe, the camel and the cat are the only animals that have a gait that moves front and hind legs together first on one side, then the other.

Cats are also the only clawed creatures that walk on their claws, not on their paws.

Interestingly, in the northeastern United States cats are frequently born with six or seven toes on one paw.

Most of the time, cats do land on their feet

Each year, hundreds of cats fall from high tree branches, roofs of houses or open windows of high-rise apartment buildings – and yet most of them manage to survive relatively uninjured. Although for centuries there have been monstrous children who have tested the hypothesis that cats will always land on their feet, serious researchers have recently discovered that cats falling from as many as thirty-two storeys have the ability to 'parachute' safely to the ground by spreading their legs and arching their backs, thereby evenly distributing the points of impact and lessening the likelihood of serious or fatal injury.

A few years ago, a pregnant cat named Pat was accidentally knocked off a high bridge in Portland, Oregon. She not only survived the fall, but gave birth to a healthy litter of kittens a few days later.

That's not a moustache your cat wears, so don't trim its whiskers

You should never trim your cat's whiskers, even if you think they're too long to suit your aesthetic criteria. Your cat uses those whiskers to find his way in the dark and to determine whether or not he can get into – and out of – a tight space.

Let's settle the old argument once and for all: cats do not need to be bathed

There is a very good reason why the cat naturally avoids water, and the well-intentioned bathing of your cat can prove to be harmful. Soaps and detergents may remove its natural oils, and if the cat should become chilled during a bath its resistance to infection is lowered.

The cat is so fastidious by nature that the average feline spends at least 30 per cent of its waking hours grooming itself with its own moist tongue.

Correction: not all cats avoid water

That's right. The Van cat, a breed native to Turkey and rarely seen outside that country, loves to swim.

Scratch my back, and I'll scratch yours

When your cat rubs itself against your leg, it is not only making friendly contact and massaging its back against your ankle bone, it is trading scents with you. That way, you become more cat-like, and your pet feels that it has become more human.

Your feline friends are not finicky if they take a long time smelling their food

Cats also use their noses as their thermometers. If they take a while sniffing that bowl of warm milk you've just served, you probably made it too hot, and they are just waiting for it to cool down to avoid a burnt tongue or mouth.

Please, no sweets for your feline sweetie!

At least not chocolate. Chocolate may be the flavour you're prepared to die for, but it can be fatal to your cat. For one thing, the popular sweet contains oxalic acid, which prevents calcium absorption, and it contains the chemical theobromine, which is toxic to cats.

Never give your cat two aspirins and call the vet in the morning

Aspirin is poison to your cat.

Your dog's favourite food can make your tabby go blind

Don't try to economize by feeding dog food to both your canine companion and your cat. Dog food lacks taurine, a substance that is necessary for your feline friend's eyesight and healthy heart.

You say that you keep finding cat hair everywhere?

Maybe cats are basically nocturnal creatures because they shed more in the light. Your cat companion will lose more hair in the summer, of course. But be advised that electric light also causes the hair to fall out – and that includes the illumination from your television set.

Not every cat is warm and friendly

Animal researchers have determined that about 15 per cent of all kittens will resist domestication and socialization with humans.

Interestingly, such felines are not the flighty, tempera-

6

mental ones, but the ones in the litter who appear very slow and quiet.

You listen; I'll talk

Cats have always made good listeners, especially as they sit on your lap being petted. A recent survey discovered that only 5 per cent of all cat owners do *not* talk to their feline pets.

THE CROWN FOR THE WORLD'S HEAVIEST CAT

No tubby tabby has yet beaten the record set by Himmy, an Australian cat, who tipped the scales at 45 pounds 10 ounces in 1982.

In 1991, the US tabloid *National Enquirer* conducted a contest to determine the heaviest cat among its millions of readers. The winner was Spike, the 37-pound 13½-ounce tabby owned by Gary Kirkpatrick of Madrid, Iowa.

In 1992, the *National Examiner*'s 'Fattest Cat in America' contest located Morris, the tubby tom-cat owned by Fred and Jeannie Scott of Ottawa, Kansas, who weighed in at a hefty 36 pounds. The runner-up in the competition was Tiger, a 33-pound brown tabby belonging to Paul and Teri Hammer of Excelsior, Minnesota.

And before we leave consideration of size to go on to another topic, it should be mentioned that the World's Smallest Breed is the Singapura, a street cat that lives in drains in Singapore.

THE WORLD'S RICHEST CATS

Nicodemus lived a true ugly duckling story. The unwanted runt of a pedigree litter, Nicky grew to be the glamorous snowy-white Persian who became a famous model for Revlon cosmetics.

In the 1960s, Nicodemus went on to become a cottage industry, and the sophisticated cat even guested on the *Today Show*, *Captain Kangaroo*, *Play Your Hunch*, and many other US television shows.

When Walt Disney was looking for a cat to co-star in the film *Incredible Journey* (1963), veteran animal trainer Al Koehler went on a 'talent hunt' to the Chafee Humane Association Pound in Ontario, a suburb of Los Angeles. It was here that he bought the Siamese that Disney himself came to name Syn Cat, 'because he synchronizes so well with everything'.

Syn Cat was decreed by Koehler to be 'the smartest, most sociable, most emotionally stable cat in the world'. Proclaiming the affable Siamese to be a cat that turns up only once in a lifetime, Koehler saw Syn Cat go on to star in other memorable Disney films, such as *That Darn Cat* (1965) with Hayley Mills and Dean Jones.

In the early 1960s, two fifteen-year-old cats, Hellcat and Brownie, were left nearly $500,000 from the estate of Dr William Grier of San Diego, California.

About the same time, a white alley cat named Charlie Chan was left the entire estate of his owner, Grace Alma Patterson of Joplin, Missouri. Mrs Patterson stipulated in her will that when Charlie died the three-bedroomed house, the seven-acre pet cemetery, and the $1/4-million antique collection were to be auctioned off and the proceeds donated to local and national pet charities.

On 25 July 1991, Damon and Pythias, a pair of six-year-old Burmese, inherited the $750,000 Fifth Avenue co-op of widowed millionairess Terry Krumholz. Further stipulation in the will required cat caretakers to perform on a regular basis such duties as the administration of hair-ball medication and the providing of proper toys for the wealthy pets.

Muriel Fletcher wanted to be certain that her beloved Blackie would be well cared for after her death, so she left her cat a fortune of $100,000. When she passed on in 1991, Blackie was able to take up residence in a plush cattery owned by Don and Mimi Cottrell.

Blackie was already acquainted with the Cottrells, for it was they who had looked after the cat when Muriel went on her annual holidays. They pointed out that although Blackie could dine on steak and salmon every meal if that were his wish, the wealthy cat preferred Little Friskies.

The Cottrells won't be adding to their own bank account when Blackie joins his mistress on the other side. Whatever cash remains will be equally divided between the Society for the Prevention of Cruelty to Animals and a local animal welfare society in Great Britain.

Eccentric miser Ben Rea, a bachelor landlord so frugal that he would wear his own tenants' cast-off clothing, died in 1990 at the age of eighty-two and left his fortune of $14 million not to one particular cat, but to three charities that supported strays.

His furious relatives didn't get a penny from the sale of his ten houses and his elegant antique collection. Not even his sixty-six-year-old housekeeper, who had looked after the old man for forty years, received a cent for her decades of devotion.

'I'm really not surprised,' said Ms Martin, Ben Rea's housekeeper. 'The only thing he cared about was cats. He only had Blackie when he died, but he had owned as many as fifteen cats at a time.'

Yet another cat named Blackie strayed on to the property of Mrs Dorothy Walker just three years before her death, and he ended up the ward of Britain's Royal Society for the Prevention of Cruelty to Animals, which will receive her bequest, running into millions of pounds, on the condition that he be given loving treatment until he journeys to cat heaven.

Although Mrs Walker had never joined the society or even contributed to any animal charity during her lifetime, she often told her housekeeper that she really thought more highly of animals than she did of human beings. In spite of her strong views, including her opinion that anyone found guilty of cruelty to animals should receive the death penalty, Mrs Walker had never owned a pet until Blackie strayed into her house one day.

In 1992, Cyrus, a seven-year-old cat, inherited a lavish, fifty-room, $850,000 mansion in Bridgeport, Connecticut, that boasts a litter box in every room. Horace Venting, the attorney for Cyrus' late owner, Beatrice Farrington, stated that his client feared that her beloved cat would be neglected by her surviving relatives, so she clarified matters by leaving her entire estate to him.

And as we leave our feline friends to enjoy their fabled riches, we will close by suggesting that all the stray cats in France have begun to purr harmoniously in gratitude for the benevolence of the elderly couple Lucien and Marcelle Bourdon, who recently auctioned off fifty-four valuable paintings and donated a mind-boggling £40 million to charities which look after abandoned cats.

CHAPTER TWO

CATS COURAGEOUS

Dr Frank S. Caprio, a psychologist and author, has stated that cat owners are healthier, happier and live longer. 'Talking to your cat,' he says, 'is one of the best stress-relief valves you can have.'

Some cat owners are healthier, happier and will live longer because their pets actually saved their lives.

Jack, a young tiger tabby, rescued single mother Corrie Owens and her five-month-old son Brandon from a fire in an apartment building in Montreal, Canada.

Minnie, a Maltese, kept working on her sleeping mistress until she awakened. The cat knew that something in the air just didn't smell right, and Mrs Rose Daigle managed to get out of the gas-filled room, thus avoiding the ultimate sleep.

In Modesto, California, Oscar saved four-month-old Anthony Phillips from choking to death in his cot.

TRIXY RANG THE BELL AND BROUGHT HELP FOR HER INJURED OWNER

On 8 December 1977, a small brown Abyssinian named Trixy was responsible for bringing aid to her injured owner, W. A. Bigelow of Shawnee, Kansas.

Bigelow had fallen on the concrete path in front of his

home and had broken his hip. Unable to move, the seventy-nine-year-old man lay helpless in his pain. His feeble cries for help failed to elicit any type of response from his nearby neighbours.

Then his cat Trixy bounded into view. Cocking her head quizzically from side to side, Trixy seemed to be thinking the situation through very carefully.

'I need . . . help. I can't . . . get up,' Bigelow managed to force past his pain. Then a wry, ironic chuckle broke through his agony as he reminded himself that he was talking to a cat. What did he expect Trixy to do? Carry him into the house and call an ambulance?

Trixy began to pace nervously around the form of her fallen owner. Suddenly her attention seemed to be directed to an outside dinner bell, a remnant of an earlier, happier time in Bigelow's life – a time when his late wife and he were younger and their children were still at home.

The dinner bell! Bigelow groaned inwardly. He had only recently tied the rope up out of the cat's reach so that she might not playfully tug at it and annoy his neighbours by ringing the bell.

The height of the rope seemed not to be a relevant factor in Trixy's intense planning. Although she had not attempted to ring the bell since her master had scolded her and tied the rope up out of her reach, Trixy seemed to be considering that, in the light of the present emergency, all would be forgiven if she were to make the bell ring for all it was worth.

Trixy leaped a good three feet into the air and managed to grip the rope with her teeth, thus bringing forth a resounding gong from the bell.

Stubbornly, the little Abyssinian kept her jaws clamped tightly round the rope and swung her weight from side to side, vigorously ringing the bell. Twice Trixy lost her hold on the rope and had to make the jump all over again – but she triumphantly rang the bell again and again.

It seemed as though she was justifiably proud of herself when the first of the neighbours came running to see what was wrong and found her owner lying on the path.

In hardly any time at all, someone had called an ambulance and Mr Bigelow was on his way to hospital and professional medical attention.

While he recuperated in the hospital, Bigelow's son and daughter-in-law cared for Trixy in a manner that befitted a true heroine.

SLUGGISH 20-POUND TABBY PROVED TO BE MORE THAN A MATCH FOR THE GERMAN SHEPHERD THAT ATTACKED A FIVE-YEAR-OLD BOY

Five-year-old Jimmy Pickett of Boise, Idaho, was on the very brink of driving his mother Melinda insane. Early that September morning in 1989 the weather had been cold and rainy, and Jimmy had had to stay inside to watch television and to colour in his *Little Mermaid* colouring book. Now that the sun was out and drying up the puddles, the two-legged concentration of perpetual motion wanted to go outside and play on the tyre swing that his dad had hung from the low branch of the maple tree in the backyard.

'Can Godzilla come with me?' Jimmy asked, referring to the four-year-old red tabby that had grown from a sickly, under-sized kitten to a hefty 20-pound feline. Godzilla had originally been christened Sammy, but when he just kept growing and growing to monster size, Melinda's husband Jack had come up with an appropriate nickname.

'Try and keep Godzilla inside the house when you go out to play,' Melinda laughed. The big cat loved to be with Jimmy, but had become so sluggish and lazy that it would probably just curl up near the maple tree and take a nap in the sun.

'Now remember,' Melinda shouted a reminder after her son as he bolted out through the screen-door, 'don't either you or Godzilla tease Geronimo!'

The Lober family next door had a fourteen-year-old

German shepherd named Geronimo that had recently become cross and mean. It seemed as though the very sight of Godzilla would send the dog into a feeding frenzy, and sometimes Jimmy's shouts and laughter would get on its nerves.

Godzilla had a mischievous streak of his own that, in spite of his sluggish bulk, would cause him to strut back and forth deliberately on the top rail of the old wooden fence, teasing Geronimo by staying just out of the dog's jumping range. The trouble was, Melinda worried, the fence was getting quite rickety and rotten. If that big German shepherd ever got upset enough over Godzilla's teasing and Jimmy's raucous play noises, he might just break the unstable wooden posts to get at them.

Melinda will probably chastise herself for ever for getting so involved in her favourite soap opera that afternoon, because she heard nothing unusual until Jimmy's screams ripped her attention from the world of television fantasy to the awful reality of her son's pain. Then her heart slammed at her chest when the sound of angry growls told her that her son's screams were broadcasting an anguish much more terrible than the pain of a skinned knee from a tumble off the tyre swing.

As she ran out of the back door, she was horrified to see that Geronimo had Jimmy down on the ground, mangling him with his massive jaws. Her son's cries tore at her maternal instinct and drove her reluctantly on towards the German shepherd.

Melinda emitted a scream of helpless rage when the big dog, which weighed at least 120 pounds, clamped his jaws around Jimmy's left arm and began shaking him as if he were a rat.

That was when Godzilla, who was normally the most gentle of cats, who was also fat and sluggish, leaped from the tree on to Geronimo's back. Godzilla's own low growl of anger and defiance replaced the dog's snarls of triumph.

Before Melinda could confront the vicious dog, it had released Jimmy with a howling yelp of pain. Godzilla had sunk his claws into the dog's back, and there was no way that

Geronimo's pain threshold could block the hurt caused by the searing, slashing razors of a 20-pound cat atop his back.

The German shepherd beat a hasty retreat into his own yard, but Godzilla did not release his hold until he had punished the brute to his satisfaction.

Jimmy was severely bitten, with numerous gaping wounds dangerously near his eyes and jugular vein. As Melinda scooped up her son in her trembling arms, she knew that he would require many stitches and hospital care – but thank God and Godzilla, none of the wounds appeared to be life-threatening.

'We know that Godzilla saved Jimmy's life,' Melinda said. 'If Geronimo had been allowed to mangle him for only a few more seconds, his huge teeth might have gouged a fatal wound in his throat. The police came to get the German shepherd and to dispose of him. Something the Lobers should have done as soon as he started getting mean.

'When Jack and I got back from the hospital that day, we gave Godzilla a large plate of liver. We decided that we didn't care if he grew to weigh 50 pounds. We knew that he would always come to our rescue no matter how fat he got.'

BARTHOLOMEW'S 'NOSE-PUNCHING' SAVES FAMILY FROM FIRE

Lucille Melander of Little Rock, Arkansas, was taking a nap in her bedroom when Bartholomew, her nine-year-old Russian Blue, began to strike at her nose with his paw.

'I was startled and kind of angry,' Ms Melander says. 'I'd had Bartholomew since I was seventeen, and he had never taken such liberties with me.'

As she sat up to chase the cat off her bed, Lucille woke up enough to smell the smoke that was issuing into her bedroom.

'I jumped out of bed and looked out into the front rooms. There was a raging fire in the living room, and I saw that the best thing to do was to grab the kids and get out of there fast. My husband Danny had already left for work, so I knew I had to do it myself.'

As thick, acrid clouds of smoke began to swirl around her feet, Lucille ran into the nursery and quickly grabbed her eighteen-month-old twin girls from their beds.

'Bartholomew was right at my side,' she says. 'It was as if he had to be certain that I knew what to do in such an emergency. It was actually a good thing that he stayed with me, because the smoke was getting thicker and thicker and once, when I started to run in the wrong direction, he bit me in the ankle and directed me to safety.'

Lucille and her husband lost their new home but she had saved the lives of their daughters, as well as her own life – and that of Bartholomew.

'Bartholomew was the one who saved *our* lives,' she says. 'If he hadn't started to use my nose for a punching bag, I might well have remained sleeping until it was too late to save the girls – or myself. I had always felt that we developed a strong telepathic rapport during our nine years together. Bartholomew certainly proved his love for me and for my daughters by helping to get us out of that burning house.'

MARY POPPINS RESCUES TWO-YEAR-OLD FROM A RATTLESNAKE

Varee Reeves, a thirty-year-old mother from Mesa, Arizona, was about to join her two-year-old toddler, Gene, in their backyard when she heard what she at first believed to be the sound of a broken sprinkler.

'We had recently installed an automatic sprinkler system to water the various plants in our yard,' Mrs Reeves says. 'We had had a little trouble with the pipes bursting as we installed the system under the sand, so I thought, "Oh, no, here we go again – water is spraying out from a leak."'

But as she listened more closely, she realized that she was

not hearing the hissing of water as it escaped from a tiny hole in a pressurized pipe. She was hearing the angry and defiant hissing of their new kitty, a white Turkish Angora named Mary Poppins.

'Thinking that Gene might be teasing Mary Poppins and be cruising for a good scratching, I picked up my sunglasses and the romance novel I was reading and pushed open the sliding glass door that led to the backyard.

'I think my heart literally stopped beating when I saw a rattlesnake moving slowly towards Gene. The only thing that blocked the snake's path was Mary Poppins, who was bobbing and weaving in front of it.'

Varee grabbed the outside telephone and quickly called the police. Somehow she managed to describe the horror that was occurring in their backyard – and tell the officers to hurry!

The snake was now coiled, and its rattles were buzzing its angry and poisonous intent. But Mary Poppins refused to back down. She sat up on her haunches and met the snake's hypnotic stare with a withering glare of her own.

'It was truly as if Mary Poppins were a snake-charmer, weaving her supple white body back and forth before the fierce and deadly triangular head of the rattlesnake. She seemed to be deliberately causing the snake to focus its attention on her swaying white body and distracting it from its deadly movement towards Gene. My two-year-old son simply sat there, completely transfixed by the incredible action drama taking place before his widened eyes.'

Then a most remarkable thing occurred. The rattlesnake relaxed its coiled position and began to retreat, slowly edging itself away from the cat.

'I saw that the thing was over four feet long, and I became even more frightened than ever,' Mrs Reeves says. 'But it also flashed in my mind to wonder if somehow during their staring contest Mary Poppins had telepathically sent a frightening message to the snake that made it retreat.'

From time to time the snake would cease its withdrawal and appear to rally its courage for another try at the boy.

'Mary Poppins would be right there, standing her ground,

staring at the invader with her unblinking blue eyes,' recalls Mrs Reeves, 'and the snake would once again be forced to back away.'

Within minutes two police officers and a man from the reptile control bureau arrived. While the policemen stood on guard, the reptile handler deftly caught the rattlesnake with a looped pole and dropped its writhing bulk into a canvas sack.

'We'll take Mr Rattlesnake back out to the desert where he belongs,' an officer told Gene.

'OK. Good,' Gene finally said, nodding his head vigorously, at last breaking the spell under which he seemed to have been placed.

Varee Reeves says that Mary Poppins was rewarded with a can of top-grade cat food. 'We're thinking of renaming her, though. Maybe Wonder Woman is a better name for her after she so bravely saved Gene.'

EIGHTY-YEAR-OLD RUSSIAN'S CAT KEEPS HIM ALIVE

In the summer of 1992, the Associated Press carried an item which quoted the *Komsomolets Kubani* newspaper's account of an eighty-year-old man in the southern Russian town of Labinsk who was being kept alive solely by the benevolent actions of his cat.

According to the story – also transmitted by the NEGA news agency – the man's feline benefactor caught pigeons and brought them home to his hungry master, who proceeded to make soup with the day's catch.

Knowing full well that he had an enviable solution to the economic hardships that were staggering the nation, the elderly man sought to have his cat insured with the state insurance authorities. The cat was, after all, his sole means of support. To his dismay, the unsympathetic insurance officials turned down his petition.

The newspaper report went on to state that the man had

taken his complaint to President Boris Yeltsin, urging that elderly people on fixed incomes had been the ones hardest hit by the current economic reforms. Without the keen hunting prowess of his generous cat, the eighty-year-old man argued, he would surely starve to death.

SINBAD THE SIAMESE AND THE HALLOWE'EN MIRROR

'What is wrong with Sinbad?' Clark Henricksen asked his friend Susan Davidowicz. 'Your normally gregarious Siamese has been doing nothing for the past hour but sitting on the sofa and staring up at the plate-glass mirror in the dining room.'

Susan had no immediate explanation. Sinbad had been in Clark's apartment on several previous occasions. Today was a Saturday, and since Clark had asked her to help him decorate for a Hallowe'en party that October night in 1992, she had brought Sinbad along with her.

'Since there will only be eight of us, I want to have a sit-down dinner around the table,' Clark said, quickly diverted from the mystery of Sinbad's obsession with the large mirror. 'I'll light a fire and we can sit around telling ghost stories after we eat. The reflection of the flames in the big mirror ought to really heighten the eerie effect.'

Susan found herself laughing out loud. 'Perhaps there's already a ghost here. I mean, the way Sinbad keeps staring at the mirror over the dining-room table. Isn't there some old legend about a cat looking into a mirror on Hallowe'en?'

Clark opened a box of orange and black streamers for the ceiling. 'I believe you're thinking of a sweetheart looking into a mirror on Valentine's Day and seeing an image of her future mate,' he said in a less-than-excited tone of voice.

Susan shrugged. 'Maybe. But isn't there another old legend about looking into a mirror and seeing ghosts standing behind you?'

Clark sighed as he handed her a roll of tape and a handful of crêpe-paper streamers. 'Perhaps you saw that in the motion picture *Freddy Krueger Meets Frankenstein and the Wolfman on Elm Street*,' he teased her.

Susan laughed good-naturedly at his friendly mockery, but she knelt on the sofa beside her pet. 'What is it, Sinbad? You know something about that mirror, don't you? Come on, old buddy, you know you can tell me. What is the deep, dark secret of the mirror above Clark's dining-room table?'

Susan was about to bend her ear to Sinbad's mouth and pantomime a whispered revelation, when the Siamese emitted an incredibly loud and pitiful wail that so startled her she nearly fell on to the floor. She recovered just in time to see the heavy plate-glass mirror pulling away from the dining-room wall.

'Clark! Help!' she shouted as she managed to catch the mirror in mid-air and steady it safely against the back of the sofa. Within seconds Clark was at her side to receive the brunt of the large mirror's great weight.

After several frantic telephone calls, Clark remembered a repairman who owed him a favour; he agreed to come to the apartment to fix the mirror before the Hallowe'en party began. The repairman said that the mirror had probably been loose for months, and it could have come crashing down at any time.

'Good lord, Susan,' Clark exclaimed after the repairman had left. 'Don't you just hate to think what could have happened if that mirror's one hundred pounds of glass had shattered on us as we sat around the dinner table tonight!'

Susan nodded her quiet assent, then added: 'Thank heavens for Sinbad. It's obvious that he managed somehow to tune in to the loose mirror, and he just sat there staring at it, trying to warn us.'

'He did a good job of it,' Clark agreed. 'Especially that wail, like a tormented Hallowe'en spirit from hell.'

Susan smiled. 'And now we truly have a Hallowe'en legend to tell people – about Siamese cats and mirrors.'

SNOWBALL SAVED INFANT FROM DEATH BY STRANGULATION

Paula had acquired Snowball, a white Persian, four years before she married Stanley Wiggs. Fortunately, Stan had no grievance against cats, and the three of them moved into a new apartment in Akron, Ohio.

'I was a little concerned when the baby came along a couple of years later,' Paula admits. 'By then I had had Snowball for nearly seven years; I was afraid that he might be jealous and do something to hurt our son, Keith. I mean, you hear all those old wives' tales about cats sucking the breath out of babies.'

Once again Snowball proved to be a loyal companion to his mistress, and his only response to the infant seemed to be the expected bit of cat-like curiosity. But when Keith was about nine months old, Snowball proved that he could be more than a faithful pet – he could also be a life-saver.

Paula remembered that she was in the kitchen of their apartment chopping vegetables for a traditional beef stew, one of Stan's favourite dinners.

'Snowball started howling at the top of his lungs, which really startled me because normally he is a very quiet cat. The only time he ever yowled or fussed was if his litter box somehow got pushed into the kitchen closet and the door got accidentally closed.'

Paula thought the irritating howling would soon cease, but Snowball continued his unappreciated solo performance.

'What do you want?' she shouted, expecting him to come running at her call. In a moment Snowball's big white head would peek round the corner, the yowling would stop and the mystery solved.

Snowball did not appear as Paula had anticipated, but she continued chopping vegetables for the stew, intent upon fixing dinner, trying her best to ignore Snowball's caterwauling.

'Be quiet, you monster!' she yelled at her noisy pet when his screams reached an even greater intensity.

In retrospect, Paula knows that she should have realized at once that something was wrong.

'Snowball was usually so quiet. Such unrestrained screeching was definitely not his style. It was just that I was so damned intent upon making that beef stew taste like the kind Mom used to make.'

Finally Snowball's cries reached a pitch that could no longer be ignored.

'You'd better have a very good reason for all this, buster,' Paula growled as she headed in the direction of Snowball's wails.

For the first time she realized that the cries were coming from Keith's room. She broke into a run, fearing that something terrible was taking place in that beautiful little blue-wallpapered nursery.

'When I entered the nursery I was horrified to see that Keith had somehow pulled his mobile down from the edge of the cot and had become tangled in its cords. The more his tiny arms and legs had jerked and kicked to free themselves, the more they had drawn the strings tighter and tighter.

'Keith could not cry out his pain and frustration because one of the cords had become wrapped around his neck and was slowly choking him!'

Paula swept the containers of powder and the disposable nappies off the changing table as she desperately sought the nail cutters. She quickly freed her son from the ensnaring mobile cords that would surely have soon ended his appointed time on earth.

'As I stood there holding Keith in my arms, feeling my heart pound anxiously in my chest and watching my baby taking in deep breaths, Snowball jumped up on to the ledge of the cot rails and began to nuzzle against me. It was as if he were saying, "Boy, hon, that was a close one. If you ever hear me yelling again, you come running right away!"'

When Stanley came home that night and heard of the close call with his infant son, he made a hero badge for Snowball out of gold-coloured tin foil and pinned in to his collar.

'Snowball was a true hero that day,' Paula says. 'I will

never forget what he did, and I will be for ever grateful for the gift that he gave us when he saved our son's life.'

ELVIRA KEPT A HALF-NAKED BABY FROM FREEZING TO DEATH

Greg Harding deliberated for days before he decided to buy a cat for his seven-year-old daughter. He had just been able to afford to move his family to a quiet suburb of Seattle, and he thought it would be nice if Kimberly had a pet.

Greg had lost several cats when he was a boy. He would just begin to grow attached to them when they would either wander off and never return or they would meet with fatal accidents on the street in front of their home. He had come to consider cats as very unstable, unreliable, perfidious creatures – who were also very accident-prone.

When he brought home Elvira, a young black female, he had a little talk prepared in order to protect Kimberly's feelings. He told her that cats were like visitors, rather than members of the permanent family. Cats should be treated with love and respect, but one should never expect them to stay for very long. Therefore, she should not be hurt or take it personally if Elvira just upped and disappeared one day.

As the months went by and Elvira proved to be a regular homebody and a wonderful friend to Kimberly, Greg began to wonder if the jinx he had always experienced with cats had at last been broken.

'Elvira has brought Kimberly so much happiness,' Karen, Greg's wife, said to him one evening. 'I'm so happy that you were able to rise above your own childhood disappointment in cats. You remember I used to tell you about Tom-Tom, a cat that we had in our family for nearly twenty years.'

Greg felt he might have been guilty of some terrible self-fulfilling prophecy on the night Elvira failed to return home. He stood quietly at the door of Kimberly's bedroom as she asked in her evening prayers that Elvira please come home to her. Greg knew well the pain that his daughter was experiencing and a small voice in the back of his mind kept nagging: 'I told you so. Cats never stay.'

That night the temperature dropped, and although it seldom snowed heavily in the Seattle area, there was enough of the white stuff piled on the ground to cause Kimberly additional concern for her cat.

'Elvira will freeze to death, Daddy,' she said, fighting back her tears the next afternoon when she had returned from primary school. 'We have to find her.'

Greg knew that locating a straying cat would be no small job in their area, which was still in the process of being transformed from farms and orchards to houses and gardens. There were, in fact, numerous partially collapsed and rapidly deteriorating barns and outbuildings awaiting the quick and efficient destruction of the bulldozer. Elvira could be holed up in any one of a hundred places – or she could have been killed by traffic, an unleashed dog, or one of the raccoons that stubbornly hung on to their rapidly vanishing turf.

'Please, Daddy, we have to go out and look for Elvira!'

Is there a father with heart so dead that he can resist the pleas of his beautiful, seven-year-old daughter, the apple of his eye?

Karen saw to it that they were both well bundled against the cold and the small banks of accumulated snow, and father and daughter set out against the growing darkness in search of their missing cat.

In spite of Greg's growing scepticism, after about five minutes of Kimberly's plaintive calling of Elvira's name, there seemed to be answering 'miaows' from an old, collapsing barn.

He had to maintain a firm grasp on his daughter's hand to keep her from running on ahead. He could not risk her stumbling over snow-covered debris or stepping on a rusty nail.

When the two of them finally located Elvira, it would be difficult to determine which of them was the most startled.

The black cat had wrapped her furry body around the half-naked body of a very small baby girl.

'See, Daddy,' Kimberly smiled through her tears of joy, 'Elvira wasn't being naughty by staying out all night. She was taking care of the baby!'

The doctors at a nearby clinic agreed that the deathly pale baby would surely have frozen to death without the cat's constant attention.

The abandoned child, only a few months old, had been kept alive by Elvira's body heat and by her vigorous licking. Baby Doe was on the very edge of suffering from exposure, the doctors said, but because of the cat's intervention she would recover without any complications.

'Elvira is a heroine, isn't she, Daddy?' Kimberly asked on the way home from the clinic as she hugged the purring cat close to her. 'She couldn't have come home if she was going to save the baby girl's life!'

Greg readily admitted that Elvira would surely be forgiven for staying out all night without checking in. 'Elvira is a heroine,' he agreed.

CARAMEL AND BOBBY — TOGETHER AGAIN

Sue Blocher will always remember that day in September 1977 when her four-year-old son Bob came running up to her in the kitchen where she was busy baking oatmeal biscuits and asked breathlessly, 'Please, Mommy, oh, please! Can it sleep with me?'

As usual, Bobby was more compelling than the biscuits she was making – or anything else for that matter. He never failed to captivate her. He was something else, truly.

'Can *what* sleep with you? Big Bird? Kermit the Frog? Miss Piggy?'

Bobby laughed that deep-in-the-tummy giggle of his. 'No, Mommy, no! My kitty. Can my kitty sleep with me tonight?'

Sue arched an eyebrow, wiped a piece of oatmeal biscuit dough from the edge of the bowl where it was about to drop to the floor.

'But, Honey Boy,' she said in a gentle but puzzled tone, 'you don't have a kitty.'

'I do now, Mommy,' he replied confidently. 'A pretty caramel-coloured kitty, just like before. Daddy is bringing her home to me. I saw him buy it.'

Darn it! Sue's smile became something more like a grimace. Bobby was always doing things like this to her. What did he mean, 'a caramel-coloured kitty just like before'?

And did he really *see* Edward buying him a cat?

Well, she would know the answer to the latter question very soon. Her husband was due home from Boston a little after five p.m.

Bobby went out to play, and Sue went back to creating Massachusetts' most marvellous oatmeal biscuits.

At 5.08, Edward pulled into their driveway with the furry and animated answer to whether or not Bobby had seen Daddy purchasing a cat.

Neither Sue nor Edward had ever seen their son so elated. They were touched by his tearful thank yous, but strangely puzzled by his triumphant shout: 'Oh, yes! It's Bobby and Caramel – together again!'

In the next few weeks, it certainly seemed as though they truly were 'together again' – boy and kitten were seldom apart. And they did sleep together every night.

In December, when Gail, his baby sister, was born, Bob and Caramel were at the door to be the first to greet her when Sue and Edward brought her home from the hospital.

Gently nudging Grandmother Linzer aside, Bob beamed and said to his cat, 'See, Caramel. Little Gail. Just like before.'

Edward and Sue exchanged puzzled glances; and later that evening, while they sat at the dinner table talking over the excitement of the day, Sue asked what Bobby had meant by 'Just like before'.

Bobby shrugged, moved the tip of his left forefinger

through a spot of gravy on his plate. 'Like before. You know, like before when Caramel, Gail and I were together.'

Edward laughed at his ever-imaginative son, but his mother-in-law glowered at all of them.

'Such silly talk!' Grandmother Linzel expressed her disapproval. 'Susan, I've warned you before that you should not permit Robert to chatter on so about such nonsense.'

'Mother,' Sue reminded the older woman, 'Bobby won't be five for another six months. He's a little kid, Mother. Little kids sometimes say weird things.'

'You never did,' she sniffed. 'And remember, as the twig is bent, so grows the branch.'

As they were preparing for bed, Sue, in her fatigue and stress with the new baby, asked her husband tumble-tongued to pass her the baby *chowder*, rather than the powder. Edward teasingly reminded Sue that she never said 'weird' things.

Sue laughed, happy for the release of tension. She agreed with her mother's observation that she had been a perfect child, then, seriously, asked her husband what he made of Bobby's frequent referencees to 'like before' – first with Caramel and now with his new sister.

'Perhaps he had wanted a cat for so long and so badly that it seemed to him as though he had already had the cat when I finally did bring it to him, and maybe the same thing is true about Gail,' Edward managed without taking a breath. 'Or maybe it is as you said: "Kids say weird things."'

Life proceeded on its normal, hectic course in the Blocher household in a quiet suburb of Brookline, Massachusetts. Edward received another promotion and things became more comfortable and less chaotic. Although there was still not enough extra money to allow for more than an occasional night out, Sue did not mind, for she really hated to leave her young children in the care of a babysitter.

The relationship between Bobby and Caramel had achieved almost preternatural proportions, and Sue was convinced that boy and cat communicated on some telepathic level beyond the ordinary.

At first she had been worried that the tight union between Bobby and Caramel would not bear an intruder, but her fears proved unwarranted. Both Bobby and Caramel appeared to adore Gail, and they played with Baby Sister whenever Mommy permitted.

It was just before Bobby's seventh birthday that Sue and Edward's universe became quite a bit larger than its previous parameters.

At a quarter to three in the morning, they were both awakened by their son's sobbing and weeping. His cries were such that both of them responded.

'I don't want Caramel to die,' he said between convulsive sobbings. 'I don't want her to die again!'

The cat looked up at them from its makeshift nest in Bobby's bedspread. Its large green eyes appeared to glow in the dim illumination from the Donald Duck night-light near the bedroom door.

'Caramel is fine, Slugger,' Edward said softly. 'You were just having a bad dream.'

'No.' Bobby shook his head. 'Tomorrow I'll be seven. I don't want Caramel to die like before.'

'Bobby, what is this "before" business again?' Sue wanted to know.

'Like before when the wolf tried to eat Gail! Caramel and I fought and fought to save her, but the wolf killed Caramel – and nearly killed me!'

Edward shook his head and laughed. 'Wow! My man, what did you have for a snack before you went to bed? Whatever it was, you are never eating it again!'

Sue stayed at Bobby's bedside, holding his hand until he went back to sleep.

The next afternoon Sue was in the kitchen frosting the birthday cake for Bobby's party. Her mother was in the backyard with Gail and Bobby. Edward was still at work, but expected home at any moment. At 5.30, the Murchisons and the Quateros and the Fanellis would be bringing their children for Bobby's birthday party. In her mind, everyone was accounted for, and her world was an orderly place.

What she hadn't counted on was the large German shepherd that had somehow entered their yard.

'Shoo, you dog!' Sue heard her mother scolding. 'You don't belong in here, you nasty thing! Get out. Shoo! Shooo!'

Then, as she watched in horror through the kitchen window, she saw the German shepherd lunge at her mother. Grandmother Linzer screamed, stepped backwards, and tripped over one of the benches by the picnic table.

In her terror and confusion, Grandmother Linzer dropped Gail.

Sue's mouth opened in a silent scream of anguish as her worst nightmare came to life – and she seemed helpless to do anything to stop it. In absolute dread she watched the German shepherd moving towards Gail as if someone had thrown it a tasty chunk of meat.

And then, as if from out of nowhere, Caramel was on the big dog's muzzle, scratching, hissing, biting – a veritable guardian angel with claws.

And Bobby was there. Her beautiful, valiant, seven-year-old son was striking at the monstrous dog with the little red plastic baseball bat that he had recevied on his sixth birthday.

Against what would seem impossible odds, Bobby and his cat were bravely allied to protect the baby that lay helpless on the ground beside the picnic table.

'Not like before! Not like before! Not like before!' Bobby chanted in rhythm to the stinging swats that he delivered to the snarling behemoth that threatened his sister.

Bobby's words from the night before echoed in Sue's brain: '*We fought and fought to save her from the wolf!*'

My God! Could it be true? Were Bobby and Caramel fighting the 'wolf' all over again.

Bobby and Caramel – together again!

The huge dog shook its head vigorously and sent Caramel flying against the side of the house. The cat was dazed from the blow, but it rolled to its feet and once again advanced against the intruder.

Somehow Bobby had got astride the dog and was pulling both of its ears with all his strength. The distraction was all

Caramel needed. This time she went for the giant's eyes. She was a demon out of hell, as well as a guardian angel.

The German shepherd flipped Bobby, got the boy on his back, and tried to sink its fangs into his throat. Bobby cried out in pain as the dog's vicious teeth tore pieces of flesh from his chest.

Her master's screams brought a frenzied power to Caramel's attack. Mercilessly, she sunk steeled claws into the dog's left eye.

Amidst terrible yowls of pain, the dog tried desperately to shake the screaming cat from its face and save its eye.

By the time Caramel had once again been thrown against a wall, it no longer mattered. Sue was there with a frying pan, and as if the feline fighting spirit of Caramel had possessed her, she struck at the big dog's head again and again with the heavy iron utensil.

The German shepherd was dazed, bewildered, barely alive when it staggered from the Blochers' yard. Within the hour, an animal control unit had it in custody.

Bobby missed his birthday party. He had to have some stitches and a few injections. Caramel had a broken back leg that had to be set and placed between splints. But baby Gail was uninjured. Grandmother Linzer was unharmed.

And as Bobby said as he hugged his cat on the way home from the vets', 'Bobby and Caramel. Together again!'

Neither Sue nor Edward asked what he meant. Whether their son had some memory of a past-life event or whether he had experienced a kind of symbolic premonition of the future, it really didn't matter. They only knew for certain that love – whether between humans and humans, or between animals and humans – lasts for ever.

CHAPTER THREE

KITTY, COME HOME!

Cookie found herself shipped 550 miles away from her home in Chicago to Wilber, Nebraska, by railway express. Six months later, she managed to find her way back to her old stomping grounds in the Windy City.

Chat Beau required four months to hike the near 300 miles between his owners' former home in Lafayette, Louisiana, to the new house in Texarkana, Texas.

Pooh needed the same amount of time to cover the 200 miles between his human family's former residence in Newnan, Georgia, and their new domicile in Wellford, South Carolina.

Smokey probably rested here and there on his journey from the old homestead in Tulsa, Oklahoma, to the family's new place in Memphis, Tennessee, for it took him a year to conquer those 417 miles.

Tommy required a year and a half to do it, but he somehow managed to travel his way back home to Seattle, Washington, from Palo Alto, California – a distance of 850 miles.

LI-PING WOULD NOT BE LEFT BEHIND

Vivian Allgood, a registered nurse, moved from Sandusky, Ohio, to Orlando, Florida, leaving her beloved Li-Ping behind in the care of her sister.

Months later, to Ms Allgood's total astonishment, Li-Ping walked up to her door. The bedraggled cat had somehow managed to travel hundreds of completely unfamiliar miles to find his mistress in a state, neighbourhood and home that he had never seen.

THEIR DARLING CLEMENTINE LEFT THE FARM IN NEW YORK TO FIND HER FAMILY IN COLORADO

When Clementine's human family moved to Denver, Colorado, she was left behind on the farm outside Dunkirk, New York, because she was about to become a mother.

Three months later, her coat rough and matted, her paws cracked and worn, her bushy tail dwindled to a rag, she arrived at the front door of the family's new home in Denver.

How the loving and loyal Clementine had managed to negotiate rivers, mountains and prairies to find her way to a strange house in a city she had never been to remains a mystery.

BACK HOME AGAIN IN INDIANA

When an army sergeant from Kokomo, Indiana, was transferred to a base near Augusta, Georgia, he decided to take his faithful yellow tom-cat with him. However, the cat did not take to its new environment, and it disappeared almost as soon as the two of them arrived on the base. The career soldier spent as much time as he could searching for his pet, then disappointedly shrugged off his loss as one of the fortunes of military service.

Three weeks later, the sergeant was astonished to receive a call from friends back in Kokomo informing him that his yellow tom-cat was hanging out around his former home.

That the cat had made the return trip so quickly was all the more remarkable to the sarge's friends when he told them that the critter could not have remembered the route, because he had made the trip to Georgia shut up in a box on board an express train.

MAYBE THEY SHOULD HAVE EXPLAINED TO SATIN ABOUT THE MOVE

When the Tialas moved from Towanda, Pennsylvania, to Forest Lake, Minnesota, a most tragic thing occurred. Satin, the object of extreme amounts of affection for twelve-year-old Sylvia, escaped from his cage during the family's stay at a motel in Illinois en route.

They searched the adjacent cornfields for three hours before they convinced the tearful Sylvia that they must resume their drive to Minnesota. At that time they had no idea that Satin was not really lost, she had decided to return on her own to Pennsylvania.

Many times that winter, the Tialas were saddened to discover their daughter sobbing inconsolably over the loss of her beloved Satin.

Months later, however, a former neighbour called them with the remarkable news that Satin had returned to their former house in Towanda. The stalwart cat had accomplished his 800-mile odyssey in about eleven months, but he shunned the old neighbours and resisted all their efforts to care for him. And while Satin would not accept charity, neither would he leave the premises.

The Tialas made the trip back to Towanda to reclaim their wandering Ulysses and to establish him once again as the king of the household and the master of Sylvia's affections.

TOM HOLDS THE LONG-DISTANCE RECORD — 2500 MILES TO FIND HIS HUMAN FAMILY'S NEW HOME

The long-distance record for a cat finding its way to its owners' new home is held by Tom, who accomplished a remarkable 2500 miles across the continent from St Petersburg, Florida, to San Gabriel, California.

The seemingly impossible journey took him two years and six weeks – and he arrived much the worse for wear. But he cared only that he was once again united with his human family.

BUT RUSTY HOLDS THE RAPID FELINE FLYER RECORD

In 1949, a cat named Rusty caught up with his human family in Chicago after having become separated from them in Boston. Experts who have studied his homing-cat record have concluded that Rusty must somehow have found a way to hitch rides on trains, trucks and automobiles in order to have covered the near 1000 miles in just eighty-three days.

IN SICKNESS AND IN HEALTH . . .

Misele, Alfonse Mondry's cat, could not bear it when her eighty-two-year-old owner was removed from the farm and taken to a hospital in Sarrebourg, France.

What some would term a most remarkable homing instinct, others would call a miracle. Following an infallible guidance whose source as yet remains beyond the elucidation of science, Misele set out to visit Alfonse in a hospital to which she had never been. With a determination that would not yield to stone quarries, fields, forests and busy highways, she walked the nine miles to the place where medical personnel cared for her master.

Somehow avoiding the orderlies, doctors and nurses, Misele located Alfonse's room, pushed open the door and jumped on to his bed.

Later that evening, when nurses and doctors found the cat purring contentedly across the old man's legs, they listened to their hearts, rather than their trained minds, and permitted Misele to remain.

Boots was another cat who could not bear to be separated from her human, when Leonay Worley was taken to a nursing home in Davenport, Iowa, twelve miles away.

Ninety-two-year-old Leonay was delighted when Boots pushed open the door to her room, and the two of them enjoyed a tearful reunion.

For the nit-pickers who feel compelled to point out that Boots had visited the nursing home on *one* prior occasion, let us remind them that she had travelled there in a covered box.

SUGAR FOUND HER WAY HOME — IN SPITE OF TWO MOVES

When the Stacy Woods family decided to move back home to Gage, Oklahoma, from Anderson, California, they thought that it would be best to leave their cat Sugar with a friend. After all, they had moved from Oklahoma to California and now back again to Oklahoma in a brief period of time. All of this moving around, they reasoned, would only confuse their pet.

Fourteen months later, Sugar had managed to find her way back to her human family in Oklahoma.

Although he truly wanted to be a believer and welcome Sugar back to the fold, Stacy Woods just couldn't accept that she had really returned. How could a mere cat like Sugar possibly hike or hitchhike over 1400 miles and find her way back home?

But then Stacy recalled that their pet had a peculiarly deformed hip-bone from a right rear leg that had been broken in her kittenhood. He ran his hand over the feline's flank and found the deformity. The remarkable travelling cat was, indeed, their Sugar.

HOW DO THEY DO IT?

How do cats perform such incredible feats of what appears to be almost supernatural ability to zero in on their human family wherever they might be? Tales in which a cat finds its way *back* to an established and familiar home over a distance of hundreds of miles are remarkable enough, for they seem to reveal evidence of some fantastically developed homing instinct. But the accounts of fabulous felines who have traversed unfamiliar and far-distant landscapes to locate their human families in new homes seem to defy all easy explanations. Somehow the image of a tabby hitchhiking with a map under its arm just doesn't do justice to the reality of these extraordinary feats.

Of course there will always be the sceptic who decides, somewhat patronizingly, that these people have simply been accidently 'found' by stray cats looking for homes, strays that may coincidentally bear a close resemblance to the cats that got left behind.

While we cannot deny that such a rational explanation might account for an occasional case now and then, we have a considerable amount of faith in a cat lover's innate ability to recognize his or her own pet.

But we don't need to wonder about sceptical cries of 'mere coincidence' in such cases as the following.

THE WONDERFUL ONENESS OF ALL LIFE

My friends among the traditional American Indians have no problem with such accounts as the above, for they believe that all life is one. And rather than seeing themselves as having dominion over the beasts, birds and fish, they perceive all life-forms as being interconnected.

In other words, the accounts of cats who have found their way back to their human families are examples of four-legged entities simply perceiving the lines of connection to their two-legged friends and following the path that the Great Mystery reveals in order to be together once again.

'This is not "magic",' a friend of mine, who is a shaman of a northeastern tribe, explained to me. 'It is a power that you use when you have need of it. You see, we are a part of nature and everything is part of one whole. And at the same time, the whole is contained in each part. You are not only a part of the whole, but the whole is part of you.'

Traditional shamans, medicine priests, and those native Americans who follow the old ways, so revere all expressions of life that when, for whatever reason, they must cease the existence of an animal, they first utter a prayer, as if performing a sacrament. They believe that the soul of the animal and its group spirit must be told that such an act of physical death is necessary in the turning of the great wheel of life.

Because of the medicine priests' great reverence for all the Great Mystery's life expressions – animal as well as human – many early missionaries falsely concluded that the native Americans were given to the worship of idols and a hierarchy of many gods.

All those humans who live in an open and loving kinship with their pets may develop a sensitivity similar to the harmony with all life that the traditional Indian experienced. Modern science is beginning to demonstrate that there is a distinctive 'energy field blueprint' around each individual human, animal and vegetable. Because there appears to be a universality to such electrodynamic field phenomena, we may theorize that on one level of reality every single living cell may be connected to every other living cell.

In order to achieve a non-physical link-up or a mental communcation with family, friends or pets, a human may have to separate him or herself from the demands of physical reality through dreams, visions, meditation or the practice of some technique that encourages an altered state of consciousness. In such entities as cats, who deal with fewer mental, emotional and cultural demands, it may be a great deal easier to remain connected on a spiritual level with their human family.

HOWIE CONQUERED THE AUSTRALIAN OUTBACK AND 1000 MILES TO COME HOME TO HIS MISTRESS

For fifteen-year-old Kirsten Hicks the most difficult part of their long overseas family trip in 1977 would be having to leave behind her Persian cat, Howie. In fact, the only people she trusted to look after Howie were her grandparents – and they lived 1000 miles away from her home in Adelaide, Australia.

Kirsten was relieved when Grandma and Grandpa readily agreed to take care of Howie throughout the entire period of her family's absence from Australia. She knew that her grandparents had always liked her magnificent Persian, and they seemed happy at the prospect of having Howie as a house guest for the duration of her trip. The necessary arrangements were made, and for the first time Kirsten began to look forward to the long holiday with her parents.

When the Hicks family returned to reclaim Kirsten's furry friend, the grandparents hesitantly greeted them with the terrible news that Howie had disappeared. They begged their granddaughter's forgiveness, and they hoped that she would understand that they had made every effort to trace him. They felt simply awful to have betrayed her trust, but there really hadn't been anything more they could have done.

Of course Kirsten did not hold her grandparents responsible, but that did not ease her sorrow to any appreciable degree. She was heartbroken over the loss of her favourite pet.

Kirsten tried to maintain a feeble hope that Howie might still be alive, but in the honesty of her darkest moments she knew that her gorgeous Persian was really a pampered baby. Howie probably couldn't last five minutes in the streets by himself. He must have been killed by a car or a large dog.

Then, almost exactly a year later, Howie returned to the Hicks' home in Adelaide. When Kirsten's parents saw the matted, filthy, bleeding, bedraggled cat at their front door, they could not believe their eyes. The fleeting thought that the grubby, footsore Persian before them might possibly be Howie passed quickly through their minds only to be rejected. Howie was a classy, beautiful show cat, not a barely moving mud ball.

But Kirsten recognized her feline friend at once. Howie had managed to come back home to her. Doing her best to avoid irritating any of his many wounds and open sores, she picked him up in her arms amidst whoops of joy and burst into unrestrained tears when she heard his happy purring.

'Miracle' was the appropriate definition of Howie's fantastic journey. Although it had taken him twelve months to come home, the pampered Persian had somehow managed to ford wild rivers, cross hostile deserts, and fight his way through the vast wilderness of the Australian outback.

The human imagination boggles even at visualizing how the cat could have accomplished such a seemingly impossible mission. It is perhaps best to leave Howie's homecoming in the miracle category.

GRIBOUILLE MIAOWS,
'VIVE LA FRANCE!'

It was nothing personal, as Madeleine Martinet of Tannay, France, hoped her cat Gribouille would understand that day in 1987. It was just that she really could not afford to keep a cat, and her neighbour Jean-Paul Marquart was a kind man who would take good care of Gribouille.

Gribouille, we might imagine, probably shrugged his furry little shoulders in Gallic insouciance. Such things happened, after all. They were really no one's fault. The fellow Marquart set a good table. And besides, he would just be across the street so he could still look in on Madeleine from time to time to see how she was doing. Life goes on.

But a month later, Marquart upset Gribouille's catnip cart. Gribouille had no idea when he was given to Marquart that the man intended to move from Tannay to Reutlingen in West Germany!

Hold it here, my friend, Gribouille must have thought. *Deutschland* was not a part of the deal! I am a French cat through and through.

Unfortunately, John-Paul did not discuss his plans with his newly acquired cat. He packed up his family and moved to Reutlingen, over 600 miles from Tannay.

There was little Gribouille could do en route – other than complain as loudly as he could. Of course, he just got told to hush up. No one would listen to his side of the matter.

Gribouille barely took time to regain his land legs after the trip. He ate one last good meal, stuffing as much into his stomach as he dared, then set out on the return trek to Tannay.

It took the determined cat two years to conquer the 600 miles that separated him from Madeleine and his home in France.

When Gribouille reached Ms Martinet's doorstep in August 1989, he was starving, bleeding and nearly blind from a serious infection in both eyes.

Before his ragged body collapsed into her outstretched

hands, Gribouille managed to miaow his most convincing plea: 'Please, Madeleine, let me stay. Don't send me away again.'

Madeleine must have understood the full emotion in that impassioned 'miaow', for she told her neighbours that her brave Gribouille was home to stay. She would keep the courageous cat for ever.

A few doubting Thomases questioned whether it could possibly be the same cat that had left with John-Paul Marquart and his family in 1987. If it were truly Gribouille, he would have had to negotiate forests, mountains, rivers and motorways. In two years he would have been forced to endure freezing winds and rain, snow and hailstorms scorching sun and lack of food. Not to mention 1000 angry dogs and 2000 jealous cats who would have tried to eat him or put out his eyes on nearly every step of the journey.

Today, Madeleine has a cold eye and firm words for all those who would dare to deny her Gribouille his miraculous accomplishment.

'There is no doubt that Gribouille is the same cat that left Germany to return to France,' she says.

As additional proof, she cites the fact that the old mother cat that had given birth to Gribouille recognized him at once and began to lick and nurse his wounds.

'Gribouille is fit and well now,' she says. 'And he will stay a French cat for ever.'

THE RETURN OF RUSTY

Geoffrey and Sandra Langrish of Camberley, England, were not the first couple to be faced with such a dilemma. Although they were cat lovers and had owned Rusty for quite some time, they didn't know if they wanted to keep him now there was a baby on the way.

Rusty was such a loving cat, but what if he became jealous when Sandra began lavishing attention on the new arrival?

One heard all those nasty, horrid stories about jealous cats harming infants.

And then, of course, there were the hygienic considerations. Picking cat hair out of baby's feed, for example. Or what if Rusty brought home some feline disease that could be transmitted to humans? Baby would be so susceptible to such alien germs during its first few months.

Geoffrey and Sandra didn't want to take Rusty to the vet and have him put to sleep. They both knew they would suffer terrible guilt for the rest of their lives if they participated in such a deed. It would be like murder, wouldn't it? Or a sacrifice! You know, sacrificing your loving pet for the health of the baby.

Rhoda Young, who lived in the next town, heard of the Langrishes' plight and offered to take Rusty off their hands. She, too, was a cat lover and certainly didn't wish Geoffrey and Sandra to take any desperate measures.

Because they had heard about cats that wouldn't stay put in their new homes and who somehow managed to find their way back to their former owners, Geoffrey and Sandra placed Rusty in a deep basket and covered him with a thick cloth so he could not possibly see where he was going. They could tell by his nervous actions that old Rusty knew something was up, but they managed to keep him covered in the basket and blind to the world until they reached Mrs Young's home – sixteen miles away.

Geoffrey and Sandra had barely had time to exchange pleasantries with Rhoda before Rusty was out of the door and gone. It was as if he knew exactly what conspiracy had taken place behind his back, and as soon as the basket was uncovered, he ran between the humans' legs and disappeared into the village.

Things were rather tense at the Langrish household for the next few weeks. Nearly every strange sound made them glance towards the cat flap that Geoffrey had fixed in the large kitchen door, and they expected to see poor Rusty come staggering into the house, perhaps bloody and beaten, most certainly bedraggled.

And then, of course, there was the guilt. After all, Rusty had been their faithful cat. How could they have even thought to turn him out?

After a few months with no sign of Rusty, both the expectations of his return and the feelings of guilt over his disappearance began to fade. The baby came, and Sandra and Geoffrey were too busy to think very often of their cat.

And then one day, seven months later, Rusty came walking in through his special cat flap and presented himself in the Langrish kitchen. He had returned.

He was none the worse for wear, Geoffrey noticed at once. He had actually gained weight, and appeared to be the perfect picture of feline health. He was, though, very standoffish, Sandra observed. It was as if his pique at having been sent off into the world like an orphan was still very much on display.

Both Geoffrey and Sandra wondered where the rascal had been living for the past seven months. He was in much too good a condition to have been living paw to mouth in the wild. He had either been boarding with a very attractive cat lover or with a veterinarian who saw to it that he ate all the right foods, someone who kept him groomed and in excellent condition.

As might be expected, Rusty offered no comment that would clear up the mystery of his whereabouts. And the local animal experts were astounded that he had been able to find his way back home over a route he had travelled only once before – and even on that occasion he had been bundled up blind in a basket.

Rusty seemed only mildly curious about the new addition to the Langrish family, and Geoffrey and Sandra were so moved by the cat's devotion that they decided not to send him away to Mrs Young's place or to anyone else's. Rusty would have a home with them as long as he wished.

THE TRIUMPHANT HOMECOMING
OF THE PAMPERED PRINCESS

Ronald and Peggy Keaton of Grand Rapids, Michigan, made
no secret of the fact that the whole family pampered Princess,
their beautiful calico cat. After all, she was gorgeous and had
a sweet disposition, so why shouldn't everyone love her and
fuss over her?

In fact, Princess had been so sheltered that when the crisis
occurred, she had been out of the house only once in her
three-year life.

Mrs Keaton's mother, who lived in Toledo, Ohio, became
ill, and Peggy left at once with Ronnie, four, and Meagan,
two, to be at the ailing woman's side.

A few days later, Ronald and their six-year-old daughter
Stacy crawled into the van with the family dog and Princess
to drive to Toledo. Although it was only the second time in
her life that the cat had been out of the house, Ronald felt that
he could not risk leaving her at home alone.

Somewhere, between Grand Rapids and Toledo, Princess
vanished.

Ronald had made a pit stop at a highway rest area about a
hundred miles from home. He was certain that Princess was
still in the van at that time, because he distinctly remembered
he had difficulty getting back into the van because she was up
against the window on the driver's side.

Stacy got in on the passenger side and moved Princess out
of her father's way. Both Ronald and his daughter assumed
that the cat moved to the back of the van to find a comfortable
spot to take a nap.

Ronald drove straight through, and he did not stop again
until he reached his mother-in-law's home in Toledo. It was
then, while they were unpacking the van, that they discovered
that their pampered Princess had disappeared.

The three children were distraught. What would happen
to their beautiful Princess? They created frightening scenarios
of Princess's plight in their childish imaginations and the

horrid scenes managed to keep a seemingly quenchless amount of tears flowing from their reddened eyes.

In all truthfulness, Ronald and Peggy felt that their delicated house pet would not stand much chance of survival in the cruel world. After all, they kept needlessly reminding one another, Princess had only been out of the house twice in her entire life.

Certain that their beloved cat would perish in a very short time, the Keaton family forced themselves to deal with their grief over the loss of their gorgeous calico and focus upon the needs of their ailing grandmother.

It would be difficult to determine who was the most astonished when, two nights later, a neighbour back in Grand Rapids telephoned the Keatons to inform them that Princess was sitting on the doorstep of their home, impatiently awaiting their return.

Somehow a miracle had occurred, and their pampered, precious Princess had managed to walk the hundred miles back to Grand Rapids in a remarkable three days and return to the correct house. Obviously, their darling calico was made of much sterner stuff than any member of the Keaton family had been ready to acknowledge.

The neighbours promised to feed Princess and look after her until the Keatons were able to come home.

When Ronald and Peggy and the kids returned to Grand Rapids, Princess did not give them a particularly warm welcome. She seemed especially put out with Ronald. Says Peggy, 'She hissed at him!'

MIMINE SAYS, 'DON'T START THE HOLIDAY WITHOUT ME!'

Twelve-year-old Bertrand Craye found out that when you assume a close relationship with a cat, it wishes to be included in all of your plans, including your holidays.

In the spring of 1990, Bertrand's parents, Patrice and Michele, wished to visit their vacation home in Le Tourneur, France, and they thought it best to leave Mimine at home with Bertrand's older brother, Gregory.

Bertrand tried his best to explain to the two-year-old tabby that he would return soon.

'Gregory will be kind to you, you'll see,' he told Mimine. 'And I'll be back before you miss me – too much!'

But when they returned home, Gregory was forced to tell his younger brother that his pet cat had run away almost as soon as the family had left on holiday.

Bertrand was very upset. He tried hard not to show it, and he tried hard not to blame Gregory. The Craye family searched the area extensively, trying their best to locate the straying tabby. After a month, they all had to admit that Bertrand's pet was quite likely missing for good.

A few weeks later, in order to ease the pain of Bertrand's loss, they acquired another tabby and named him Mimine too.

In February 1992, Patrice and Michele returned to their country home in Le Tourneur in the company of Bertrand and Mimine II. Incredibly, they had not been there long when who should come staggering up to the front door, all skin and bone, but Mimine I!

It was apparent from the cat's bedraggled appearance that Mimine I had set out for the Crayes' vacation home nearly two years before – and had just arrived.

Somehow the persistent pussy-cat had trudged over 250 miles, across fields, forests, highways – and even the River Seine – to reach his young master in Le Tourneur. And he had finally reached his destination, twenty-two months later.

Mimine I responded to Bertrand's tender loving care and a lot of tender morsels of food. He was soon up to his old fighting weight – although he still walked with a limp, a lasting souvenir of some deadly encounter.

He even accepted the presence of Mimine II with style and sopistication. After all, Bertrand had enough love for both of them.

Mimine I had changed in one appreciable way, however. He no longer had the slightest desire to run away from home.

'PLEASE, MR BURGLAR, BRING BACK OUR BOOTSIE!'

Of course we know that some people can simply lose their minds over a cat that really appeals to them, but figure this one out . . .

In March 1992, burglars broke into an electronics speciality store in Miami and turned their noses up at expensive computer equipment, stereo units and big-screen television sets. They walked right on by top-of-the-line electronics, without touching a single piece of equipment. The sole object of their felonious quest appeared to be Bootsie, a seven-year-old black-and-white back-alley tom-cat of mixed breed.

'It's incredible,' exclaimed Benjamin Glumack, the owner of the electronics store. 'Whoever broke into my place bypassed hundreds of thousands of dollars' worth of equipment and took only Bootsie, our watch cat, his litter box, about twenty of his toys, his food dish, some snacks and his bed. And then, as if the burglars' hands got too full, they stole one of our delivery trucks to carry off all of Bootsie's stuff!'

Carmilla Schramm, Glumack's bookkeeper, says that Bootsie had become the store's mascot. 'One of us found him out in the alley all beaten and bloodied. Apparently he had just lost a fight with a pit bull or something. Ben said that we could keep him in the back room, and Bootsie had become a fixture around here for about four years.'

Glumack said that all fifteen of his employees enjoyed having the big black-and-white tom-cat around the store. 'Everybody had fallen in love with the guy. Bootsie was lovable. But who would break into the store and risk a jail sentence to steal a lovable cat?'

What puzzled employee Angelina Delpino most was the fact that Bootsie was just an ordinary cat. 'He's no expensive, pure-blooded prize-winner. He's no fancy show cat. He's just an old beat-up alley cat with only half his left ear. But we all loved him! Why would anyone steal our cat?'

Glumack admitted that employee morale really nose-dived after Bootsie was catnapped. 'As weird as it might sound,' he states, 'I don't care about the delivery truck. They can keep it if they bring back Bootsie.'

KINDHEARTED WIDOW FINED $750 FOR GIVING TWO STRAY KITTENS A TEMPORARY HOME

Can you imagine being fined $750 for feeding a couple of stray kittens? No? Well, neither could seventy-five-year-old widow Gertrude Cozard who resided in a plush Georgia suburb – and she's fighting mad.

'They can lock me up in the penitentiary if they want,' she says. 'I will not pay one cent of my fine. If taking pity on two small kittens is a crime, then they can just put me away in prison.'

Gertrude's troubles began when she spotted one of her neighbours pelting two frightened kittens with rocks. It was readily apparent that he had already struck the cats many times, and one appeared to have suffered a broken leg from the cruel treatment.

'I had always thought my neighbour to be a cold and inconsiderate person, but such outright cruelty simply appalled me. The little kittens ran towards my house and hid themselves in the bushes next to my driveway. I assumed they were strays, but that was no reason to treat them so cruelly.'

Gertrude knew that it would be against the rules of her condominium complex to keep pets, but she surely believed it would be considered only humane to give the abused kittens something to eat and not allow them to starve to death.

She put out some food by her front door, and she continued to do so for about a week. Touched by the sight of the limping kitten with its broken leg, she paid a vet over $200 to set it.

It was at about this time that she received a telephone call from a man who identified himself as one of the directors of the condominium. He told her that if she continued to feed the kittens he would walk over to her house and personally poison the cats' food.

The next few times she fed them, Gertrude stood guard over their bowls so that no cruel cat hater could spike the mix.

'Two weeks after I had begun feeding the kittens, I found them a good home with a dear friend who has always loved cats,' Gertrude says. 'I certainly considered the whole matter of the stray kittens to be concluded.'

But it was then that she received the certified letter from the condominium board demanding that she reimburse them the $750 they had spent in lawyers' fees because they had sought legal counsel on the cat-feeding matter. They demanded that she also sign a legal agreement swearing that she would never again feed another stray animal of any kind.

'Can you believe such a thing?' she asks incredulously. 'How could anyone sign such a document? Good grief, if a person cannot come to the aid of a couple of helpless kittens, then she is less than human.'

Gertrude took her story to the newspapers, and cat and animal lovers from all over the city wrote to the directors of the condominium to inform them what cruel and heartless monsters they were. Such attention, however, only seemed to enforce the board's unyielding position against Mrs Cozard.

'We're not going to let her off the hook on this matter,' one of them told reporters. 'We'll continue this fight to the very end.'

In the meantime, Gertrude hired an attorney of her own to battle the condominium board in court, and placed her $200,000 home on the market.

'I cannot live around evil people who hate animals,' she announced simply and directly.

BUT WHAT IF ALL THE KITTIES CAME HOME AT ONCE? HOW MANY CATS MAKE A CROWD?

For the first time in the history of the United States, cats are more popular than dogs.

There are an estimated 53.3 million dogs in American households and 62.4 million cats. Nearly two in five households own a dog, while one in three include a cat.

In 1991, the International Cat Association licensed 243 shows – including the largest, New York's International Cat Show held in Madison Square Garden. Dozens of others were sponsored by other cat fanciers' associations.

And while there is no question that Americans love their cats, they come in second to the people of Australia as the world's greatest cat lovers. According to *Petfood Industry* magazine, 33 per cent of all families in Australia fancy felines, followed by 30 per cent in the United States. After the US, the Canadians and the Belgians are placed third and fourth in their passion for pussy-cats.

Unlike dogs, many of whom are bred to improve their innate performance as retrievers, shepherds, watchers or guardians, cats are bred for their looks and their temperament. For cat lovers, beauty, grace and disposition are quite enough. It is not necessary for their feline pet to be able to sound an alarm, fetch downed birds, herd domesticated livestock or attack burglars.

To be a cat lover is to be enraptured by that mysterious mixture of wild beast and otherworldly being that constitutes a feline.

To be a cat lover is to hold that bizarre blend of the ethereal and the earthy in such respect that you cannot help feeling honoured when your cat jumps into you lap.

Interestingly, it would seem that even the process of breeding cats is a satisfying, almost spiritual, experience that surpasses all physical considerations – since recent statistics disclose that half of all these devoted breeders are allergic to cats.

*

To non-cat lovers, it might appear as though some people get more than a little carried away by their obsession with felines.

When Christine Ann Thomas's husband told her, 'It's either me or the cats,' the cat-loving fanatic – whose very initials spell C-A-T – did not even pause to think. She chose her cats – all 129 of them! So Billy, her husband of sixteen years, moved out of their home in Wakefield, England; and he vowed he would not return until the dozens of cats that his wife adopted hightail it out of the house.

Christine would not back down. 'By leaving, Billy has simply created more room for me to take in cats,' she said.

Jack and Donna Wright of Kingston, Ontario, own 600 cats that regularly come close to eating them out of house and home.

The Wrights were once threatened with eviction when they were unable to pay their mortgage after having spent $111,000 a year on their beloved pets. When cat lovers from Kentucky to Winnipeg learned of their plight, they rallied to the cause and sent Jack and Donna enough donations to help them regain some financial equilibrium.

Each day the Wrights feed their hosts of felines 180 cans of cat food, 50 pounds of dry cat food, and 9 quarts of milk – which adds up to $256 a day, including kitty litter. In addition, they have a vet in every day for an average of $50 a visit. That is a total of $306 a day – $2,142 a week.

The Wrights feel that every penny spent on their cats is worth it. 'We love each and every one of our cats,' they say. 'Our cats are like our children. We'll never let anyone take them away from us.'

When representatives of the Toronto Humane Society answered a call for help in the summer of 1990, they found an elderly couple in their seventies attempting to care for 160 cats in a cramped, three-bedroomed apartment.

Humane Society investigator Martha Schissler said that the couple were trying their best to care for the animals and that all of the cats were quite well fed.

'In such numbers, however, it was impossible for the elderly couple to look after them properly,' Ms Schissler explained. 'They finally permitted me to take 89 of the cats, but they insisted on keeping 71 of their favourites.'

Martha Richardson of Nashville, Tennessee, will never have to worry about her more than one thousand cats eating her out of house and home, because her precious pussy-cats are salt-cellars, dolls, statues, bookends, photographs, paintings and a seemingly endless variety of collectibles.

Ms Richardson said that she stopped counting at a thousand pieces. 'There isn't a place in my house where you can go without being stared at by a cat painting, sculpture, towel or toy cat. Every nook and cranny is crammed with cat collectibles peeking out from every corner.'

The first item she collected was a small stuffed cat doll that she was given as a child. Ms Richardson now possesses an almost endless array of cat art pieces from more than forty countries, including a cat likeness that she wears attached to her thumbnail.

It will surprise no one to learn that she sends out cat Christmas cards – with cat stamps, of course.

CHAPTER FOUR

THE TOUGH GUYS — CATS WITH MORE THAN NINE LIVES!

In the winter of 1990, Snowball, a white Angora kitten owned by Carol Gingras of Middleboro, Massachusetts, took a two-foot arrow through the head from a sick sadist and managed to recover.

In January 1990, Kelly, a once tubby tabby, owned by Rhea Mayfield of Brownwood, Texas, was found alive after having been locked in a storeroom for forty-six days without food or water – in sub-zero temperatures.

Putty Cat, an eleven-pound tom, loves to soar with the birds on a hang glider with his mistress, Patty Butler. Patty has created a special harness so Putty Cat need never miss a flight off the cliffs near Monterey, California.

In the summer of 1992, Jerry Ditzig of Highlands, Texas, was doing speed laps before going on to win the Bud Lite International Outboard Grand Prix in Missouri. When he pulled in for a pit stop, he heard a tiny mewing sound and pulled off the engine cover to investigate.

There, to his astonishment, he discovered two tiny kittens, barely three weeks old. The stowaways, one snow-white, the other black with white paws, were thoroughly soaked.

Since his wife is a 'cat nut', Ditzig decided to adopt the kittens, naming them Speed and Racer in recognition of the fact they started life doing 103 m.p.h. in a racing powerboat.

Vision, a three-year-old orange, black and white tabby, got trapped in a dresser drawer when the Williams family moved from Fort Meade, Maryland, to Lantana, Florida; and she miraculously survived an incredible forty-two days without food or water.

Prior to their departure to Florida, after Maryland movers had packed the family belongings, the Williamses had discovered that Vision was missing. After searching the neighbourhood for a week, they sadly concluded that she must have become upset by the chaotic process of moving and had run away to find a new home.

Upon their arrival in Florida, the Williams family had placed a number of items into storage, and it was a full six weeks before they were able to unpack some of the furniture pieces that they had boxed before the move from Maryland.

Poor Vision had been stuck in that dresser drawer all that time.

The examining vet said that Vision's survival was all the more spectacular when one considered that the warehouse had no air conditioning to fend off the Florida heat and humidity.

Vision had suffered some dehydration, but, according to the vet, 'She's in terrific shape for what she's gone through. We're all stunned that she was able to survive.'

Barbara Williams said that she was puzzled when she thought she heard a weak miaowing sound coming from a drawer in a dresser that they had put in storage. 'I couldn't believe that Vision was alive,' she said.

SOMETIMES A DOG'S BEST FRIEND IS A CAT

Bos'n, a large grey tom-cat belonging to the J. R. Rowntrees of Mill Valley, California, suddenly dashed from the house when he spotted their cocker spaniel Duke wandering away from their yard. Duke had gone blind with cataracts and was heading for a steep incline which would lead to a bad fall. Bos'n nudged the old dog on either side and brought him safely home.

On 17 October 1990, Teresa Harper had just let her poodle Lacy Jane out into the yard of her Dora, Alabama, home when the tiny dog was attacked by a massive pit bull that had invaded their property.

Poor little Lacy Jane was literally being mauled alive when her pal Sparky, the Harpers' cat, leaped from the roof of a nearby porch to land squarely on the head of the savage pit bull. Incredibly, Sparky, four pounds of lean, mean, fighting cat-machine, drove off the vicious dog and saved the poodle's life.

In the autumn of 1968, a tom-cat named Thug received an award for heroism from the Los Angeles Society for the Prevention of Cruelty to Animals for rescuing a dog. Thug, normally an exceptionally quiet cat, spotted a Labrador retriever being swept under a pier at a marina. The tom began a series of alarming yowls that drew attention to the dog's peril, and the Labrador, whose name was Missy, was saved.

In August 1987, a tiger-striped barn cat came to the support of her female collie friend who was desperately defending her newborn pups against the attack of a powerful and hungry predator.

Richard Olson, who maintains a large farm near Fort Dodge, Iowa, thought that Queenie, his white collie, was secure with her five new pups in an old corn crib.

'The family and I were going into town that night to see a movie,' he said. 'The girls were reluctant to leave Queenie, since she was still kind of weak and woozy from having given birth only the night before, but they fixed a nice bed for her, made up of some old worn-out blankets, and we saw to it that she was as comfortable as any mother could be who was nursing five new babies.'

When the family returned home around eleven o'clock that

night, they were horrified to see Queenie outside the corn crib, staggering and near exhaustion. In the illumination provided by the yard light, they saw splotches of blood staining her white coat.

They had little time to puzzle over what had happened, for in the next few moments something came running at her from out of the shadows and knocked her sprawling. It was a huge muskrat that must have come up from the nearby creek to get at the tender and tasty newborn pups.

'Get Dad's rifle from the kitchen closet!' Richard's wife shouted at their elder son.

Richard was afraid that it might be too late to stop the muskrat from its savage onslaught. He was too far away from the corn crib to chase the critter away, and it looked as though Queenie was down and out.

That was when another shadowy figure rose up from the doorway of the corn crib to meet head-on the determined charge of the hungry muskrat. It was Meower, their New England barn cat, and she caught the predator with a raking slash of her claws across its tender, unprotected nose.

'You could probably have heard that muskrat squeal all the way back in town,' Olson says. 'Meower stood there, poised like a prizefighter, jabbing and thrusting at the huge muskrat with drawn claws. Meower's delaying tactic gave Queenie time to regain her breath and her balance, and she got that muskrat behind its neck, shook it violently several times, then tossed it as far as she could throw it.

'The muskrat rolled about seven or eight feet into the darkness, rebounded on its feet, and came running back for another try at the puppies. It was tough and mean – and hungry for fresh meat.'

By that time Olson's son had brought him the rifle, and he nailed the attacking muskrat with three quick shots.

It didn't take the Olson family long to recreate the scenario that would probably have led to the death of one or more of Queenie's pups if it had not been for Meower's intervention.

'The grass outside the corn crib was all torn up,' Richard says. 'Queenie must have smelled the muskrat outside the crib and knew darn well the purpose of the critter's visit. Although she was weak from having given birth only the night before, she positioned herself outside to keep the invader away from her pups.

'Old Meower, who's got to be over ten years old, must have seen that her pal Queenie was getting the worst of it in her weakened condition and all, so she planted herself right in the doorway of the crib and stood there prepared to fight to the death to protect Queenie's babies. If it hadn't been for the reinforcement of Meower's sharp claws, Queenie would undoubtedly have lost a pup or two.'

IGOR THE TABBY TAKES ON TWO COYOTES TO SAVE A SIAMESE

When Connie and Dennis Junagan moved to the newly developed desert housing units outside Cave Creek, Arizona, they did not fully comprehend that in this particular region the West was still wild. Their two kids, Patti, eleven, and Bruce, nine, lived in dread of whatever might be the creepy-crawly of the day. The family cat, Igor, a large, grey tabby, suddenly found himself the possible diet of choice for a large variety of predators.

'Within the first week of our move in February 1991 we had encountered a six-foot-long rattlesnake on our driveway, a scorpion in our dishwasher, four or five lizards in our bathroom, two hairy tarantulas on our patio, a pack of six coyotes in our backyard, and a herd of thirteen *javelina*, wild pigs, in our frontyard,' Connie says. 'We were continually concerned about the kids being bitten by any one of them – and about Igor, who we feared might try to tease in a catfully playful manner some poisonous creature or other.'

On some atavistic level of instinctual longing, the mournful moon dirge of the coyotes was strangely satisfying. But then the Junagans found out just how wily those coyotes could be.

'Our next-door neighbours actually had their cocker spaniel

eaten by a pack of coyotes,' Dennis says. 'The coyotes will cleverly send a female in heat up to homes in which they can detect dogs dwelling. When the horny hound goes out in pursuit of the fertile lady, the pack of male coyotes jump him and eat him.'

The Junagans also learned that there was nothing that the coyotes loved better for a midnight snack than a cat that didn't make it home before dark.

'So many things in life present a mixed blessing,' Dennis notes. 'Although there was a definite threat to Igor, Patti and Bruce suddenly became much more responsible in terms of seeing that their pet was home safely. In our old neighbourhood in Paradise Valley they had been pretty lax about whether or not Igor was home behind doors after dark.'

Dennis commented with a wry smile that he had always known Igor to be a 'ballsy' cat, reluctant to back down before the most aggressive dogs in the neighbourhood, but somehow the big tabby had to understand that coyotes were much hungrier than the average urban mutt. As his son Bruce had phrased it, Igor's hero had always been Garfield, the pugilistic tabby in the Sunday comics.

It was Patti who actually witnessed Igor's act of heroism.

'Elise, who was nine and who lived next door, and I were playing dolly dress up with our cats in our backyard,' she says. 'Elise had pulled a pink dolly sundress on Sara, her Siamese, and I was trying to put a yellow apron around Igor's big belly. We barely had a chance to notice the two scraggly coyotes before they were right in front of our noses, growling at us and showing their teeth.'

Although their parents had warned Elise and Patti about the boldness of coyotes in wantonly invading garages and yards, it was unlikely that the adults had ever anticipated that the scavengers of the desert would have the audacity to approach humans, even little ones such as their daughters.

Patti said later that Sara, Elise's Siamese, had started yowling and hissing at the uninvited guests, but that Igor had just studied the intruders very closely, as if looking for an opening.

Sara's defiance either provoked one of the coyotes or stimulated his hunger, for he lunged at the Siamese and snatched her up in his jaws in one practised swoop. That was when Igor went into action.

'He made a really big jump and landed on the head of the coyote that had grabbed Sara,' Patti says. 'The coyote dropped Sara and shook Igor off. Then Igor went right for its face, making a terrible howling while he scratched and scratched at the coyote's nose.

'The coyote yelped so loud that both of them turned and ran from the yard. Igor was a big hero!'

Sara required a number of stitches at the vet's, but she appeared not too much the worse for wear by dinnertime that evening. Elise's parents brought Igor a can of expensive cat food as a special gift for saving their daughter's pet.

'Igor really thinks he is Garfield,' Bruce said. 'He really thinks that he can take on all comers!'

MERCEDES STOWED AWAY WITHOUT FOOD OR WATER FOR FIFTY DAYS

Although the good-natured employees at the freight company in Kent had been feeding the stray black cat bits and pieces of their lunches for the past few weeks, none of them probably thought much of it when the feline moocher stopped coming round. And it is very doubtful that any of them would have associated the disappearance of the black cat with their shipping a Mercedes-Benz car to a woman in Australia.

As remarkable as it may seem, on that day in 1990 when the employees of the freight company were in the process of sealing the metal container which was to protect the expensive car en route to Australia, they also enclosed the black cat in what might well have been her sea-going tomb.

The unwilling feline stowaway – who came to be called

'Mercedes' – survived an astonishing fifty days without food or water, locked securely in a metal shipping container.

In an unparalleled feat of endurance, Mercedes travelled 17,000 miles in her metallic crypt; and when the ship arrived in Port Adelaide, Australia, nearly two months later, customs officials were stunned when the skin-and-bone cat stumbled out of the container.

Dr John Holmden, a vet and chief animal quarantine officer in South Australia, theorized that Mercedes must have had a full stomach before she became trapped in the metal container. By licking drops of condensation and by spending nearly all of her time resting, she managed to stay alive.

When Mercedes staggered out of the container, she barely weighed four pounds. After being fed plenty of cat food and a lot of milk, she soon filled out to eight pounds, a weight that was quite likely to have been her former bulk.

Under Australia's strict quarantine laws, Mercedes had to be detained for nine months. After her release from quarantine, the owner of the Mercedes-Benz announced that she intended to adopt the feisty orphan cat who had shared the metal container with her car from Kent to Port Adelaide.

What better talisman could one possess than a living miracle cat who is able to survive odds that are one in a million?

BURIED ALIVE FOR ELEVEN DAYS, MARTY DUG HIMSELF FREE

Marty probably got himself in trouble while enjoying his favourite pastime – chasing mice into holes around the patio of the Dunbars' apartment building in Edina, Minnesota.

What probably happened on the afternoon of 9 April 1992 is that Marty got a little shy when the maintenance men came round to work on the patio, and he found a hole that was big enough for him to hide his yellow-striped tabby body. Of course Marty had no idea that the workmen would place a ten-inch slab of patio concrete over his hiding place.

Eight-year-old Frankie Dunbar was inconsolable when Marty had not come home after three days. He had received Marty on his fifth birthday, and they had become firm friends.

'I want to see my kitty again,' he sobbed to his mother, Robin. 'When is Marty going to come home?'

When Frankie's dad, Greg, returned from work on the fourth day of Marty's disappearance, the three members of the Dunbar family scoured the neighbourhood calling for the cat. Later, after dinner, they posted reward notices in all the supermarkets within a reasonable cat-hike from their apartment building.

On the evening of the ninth day, Robin and Greg placed Frankie between them on the sofa and explained about death and how, just maybe, Marty had suffered an accident and wouldn't be coming home. They both felt about one step above pond scum as counsellors when Frankie cried himself to sleep after their heart-to-heart talk.

Then, miraculously, on Easter Sunday, the resurrected Marty returned from the dead and appeared at the Dunbars' patio door.

'He was covered with dirt,' Robin says. 'His paws were so muddy it looked like he was wearing miniature boxing gloves.'

'We were nonplussed,' Gred admits. 'Speechless. We could only blurt out half-sentences like: "Look there . . . there he is . . . Marty. Look. Marty has come back."'

Although Frankie was overjoyed to see his pet returned to him from Heaven, Marty stood on few ceremonies. He headed straight for his food bowl and began to eat with what seemed to be the single-minded purpose of gaining back in one meal the apparent weight that he had lost.

When Greg and Jerry Faciana, the maintenance supervisor at the Dunbars' apartment complex, found the hole in the lawn, they began to reconstruct a possible scenario for Marty's mysterious disappearance and his miraculous return from the dead.

'We think that he must have crawled into a hole near the patio on the day the workmen were patching the area with new stones and concrete,' Greg Dunbar says. 'He probably hid from them, and they poured a slab of concrete right over the place where he lay, crouched in his hole.

'Once he realized he was trapped, Marty probably started trying to dig himself out. We figure that he must have stayed alive by burrowing into mice holes as he dug.'

Jerry Faciana commented about the condition of Marty's paws. 'The poor guy didn't have any claws left at all. He had worn them down to nothing from scratching his way to freedom.'

Frankie asked his parents if Marty had used up all of his nine lives in his escape efforts.

'Marty had always been a fighter,' Greg told him. 'I'll just bet that he saved at least one or two lives for future emergencies.'

TOM-CAT FROZEN TO A TREE RESCUED BY SIX CAT LOVERS

Teresa Bishop was on her way home from her job at a local hospital on the evening of 2 March 1991, when she stopped her car near a wooded embankment outside St Catherine's, Ontario.

'It was already dark, but I simply needed a good breath of fresh air,' Ms Bishop says. 'I had put in a really tough day, and I just needed to stop and look up at the stars and feel the chill wind against my face.'

The wind was, indeed, chilly, as the temperature was about four degrees below zero.

As Teresa stood quietly reaffirming her centre of reality in a hectic world, she heard a faint little sound, a kind of whimpering that seemed to be coming from somewhere about half-way down the wooded embankment.

Drawn by a mysterious force beyond her understanding,

she began to edge her way down through the snow-covered undergrowth. 'Even at the time I understood that I could certainly have slipped and hurt myself badly. At the very first, I couldn't quite identify what the sound was. It was now quite dark, and it took me about half an hour to pinpoint that the cries were coming from an uprooted spruce tree. After a time of hearing the cries regularly, I knew that there had to be a cat in trouble somewhere in that tree.'

Ms Bishop carefully inched herself along the trunk of the fallen tree, holding to the branches for support. Again, the thought occurred to her that she herself might fall and be injured there in the darkness. How long would it be before someone came to *her* rescue?

And then, suddenly, her groping fingers found the cat, its hind legs and tail firmly frozen to the spruce tree.

'I knew that unless I got the cat out of there in a hurry, it would soon be frozen to death. The poor thing had almost no body heat left, and with the temperature below zero, it couldn't hold out much longer.'

Desperately, she tried to dig the cat free from the ice with her fingernails.

'The ice seemed as hard as iron, and I knew that I did not have the strength to chip him free with my nails,' she says. 'The cold was starting to get to me, and I was losing my grip on the branches that kept me from falling. I knew that I would be no good to the cat or anyone, including myself, if I should slip in the darkness and lie helpless beside the tree trunk.'

Teresa climbed safely back to the road and her car, and she was soon revving up the engine to race to find additonal help to free the frozen kitty.

Officers Harry Frizzell and Al Rand followed her back to the embankment. They had both given her their promise that they would do their best to remove the cat from its prison of ice.

Officer Frizzell tried to chip the animal free with his knife, but he seemed to achieve little or no progress. Officer Rand poured anti-freeze around the cat, but that didn't work either.

Another three officers, who had been touched by the cat's

plight when they heard Officer Frizzell discussing the problem over the radio, arrived in a cruiser with two jugs of hot water.

'There were six of us there in the dark and the freezing cold when the hot water worked and thawed the ice around the imprisoned cat,' Teresa says, 'and all of us had tears in our eyes when he was free at last.'

Amidst expressions of goodwill and congratulations all round, Ms Bishop took the cat home with her.

'After several bowls of warm milk and a couple of poached eggs, his body temperature became normal,' she says, 'and that was when I knew that we had truly saved the cat's life.'

Because of the strict rules against pets that were enforced in her apartment building, Ms Bishop was unable to keep the cat she nicknamed Frosty, but she found a home for him with a loving family.

'I will always cherish the memory of that magical night when six busy humans ceased worrying about their own problems and concerns and focused their energy on saving the life of one small tom-cat that was frozen in a tree. I think we all got a good lesson in the oneness of all life that night.'

ROXANNE THE RAMBO KITTY KEEPS NEIGHBOURHOOD DOGS IN CHECK

When Michael and Elaine Claussen moved to a new neighbourhood in Albany, New York, they were astonished by the laxity and thoughtlessness of the dog owners in regard to keeping their pets in check.

'Complaining only brought apologies and promises to keep Fido on a leash,' Elaine says, 'but it just never happened.'

'The doggie-do in the yard and on the sidewalk was one thing,' Michael adds. 'The urine stains on the tyres and fence posts was another – but I planted two rose bushes, then lost them to the mutts within the first four days after we moved into the neighbourhood.'

They had lived there for only a month when their daughter Linda asked them to take care of her cat Roxanne, a crossbreed that combined a tabby and a Persian. At first the couple hesitated to assume responsibility for Linda's big brown cat. After all, the area was crawling with dogs. What if one of them injured or killed Linda's beloved companion?

'The other reason for our hesitation, quite frankly,' Michael says, 'was that I was allergic to cats. And besides that, I had never really cared for the things.'

The Claussens finally consented to take Roxanne for the next two weeks, and Linda dropped the cat off on her way to the airport.

'You'll pardon me if I leave the care and keeping of this big Mama primarily to you, dear,' Michael sniffed, reaching for his hankerchief. 'My allergy, you know.'

The next afternoon, Elaine was ironing Michael's shirts and listening to Beethoven on the stereo, when she glanced out of the kitchen window to spot a large German shepherd boldly approaching Roxanne, who was sunning herself in their backyard.

'"Oh, no," I thought to myself. "Poor Roxanne is about to be converted into hamburger,"' Elaine says. 'Michael was at work, and I was very cautious about running foul of an angry German shepherd. I was already trying to decide what I would tell Linda when she returned from her vacation.'

Roxanne barely opened her sleepily contented eyes when she reached up and expertly clawed the dog's nose with the extended claws of her left paw. The brute ran yelping from the yard like a baby that has had its hand smacked after reaching for a forbidden object.

Within a few days, it became abundantly clear that Roxanne most certainly considered herself to be a forbidden object to the teeth, muzzles or paws of any dog. The local cocker spaniels, poodles and beagles were easy knockouts for Roxanne, and she barely worked up a sweat taking out the mean Rottweiler from round the corner and the German shepherd who had come for a return match.

'It's amazing,' Michael laughed when he returned from

work on the fourth day of Roxanne's visit. 'The dogs in the neighbourhood are starting to avoid coming near our yard. Old Slugger Roxy is scaring them all away. I think I'll try planting rose bushes again.'

On Saturday afternoon, the seventh day of the reign of Queen Roxanne, Michael was able to observe their Rambo cat in action as he was stamping the soil around a freshly planted rose bush.

'This big Rottweiler approached our yard,' he says. 'I had seen the brute in the neighbourhood, and I knew that I wouldn't want to tangle with it. He walked up to the edge of our grass, and he had this low, throaty growl building in his throat.

'Without a moment's hesitation, Roxanne jumped up from where she had been napping beside me and came hissing and spitting at the big Rottweiler. The monster backed up, but then decided to stand his ground. That was when Roxy moved deftly between his front legs and sank her fangs up to the hilt in one of his back legs. The brute yelped all the way back to his own yard round the corner.'

That night, Michael gave Roxanne an extra helping of her favourite cheese and tuna food mix, then conducted a formal weighing-in on the bathroom scale.

'It might not be official,' he told Elaine, 'but our champ tips the scales at nearly twenty-five pounds. No wonder she has no fear. She knows she's the biggest, meanest pussy-cat in the valley.'

On the tenth day of Roxanne's stay with the Claussens, Elaine noticed that for the first time since they had moved to the area the dog owners were walking their pets on leashes. She also observed that most of the dogs were whimpering as they were pulled and tugged across the boundary line of their front lawn.

'Roxanne has all the neighbourhood dogs running scared,' she reported to Michael that evening when he came home from work. 'Now nearly everyone has their dog on a leash, and Mrs Myer from across the street called to see if Roxanne was inside the house before she would walk her dog.'

Michael bent down to give Roxanne an affectionate scratch behind the ear. For some reason, his allergy to cats no longer seemed to bother him.

'Roxanne is like Marshal Dillon cleaning up Dodge City,' he chuckled. 'Roxy has the fastest claws in the West.'

The next morning, when he was leaving for work, Michael was amused to see that some local wit had placed a crude 'Beware of the Cat' sign next to their front drive.

When the two weeks of Linda's holiday were completed and she stopped by their home to pick up her 'sweet little kitty', Michael told his daughter that she could have Roxanne back only if she promised to bring her over for a visit every few weeks.

THE CAT THAT WAS MISTAKEN FOR A TERRORIST BOMB

Thunderball was forced to surrender at least eight of his nine lives all at once when he had the misfortune to be sealed in a cardboard box and left in front of a US government building. The frightened feline accomplished a miraculous escape when the box was blown up by an Army anti-terrorist squad which had mistaken it for a bomb.

The terrible mishap occurred in early February 1991 during the peak of the chaos surrounding the Persian Gulf conflict. Rumours abounded that Iraqi terrorists had pinpointed numerous United States cities for reprisals, and law enforcement agencies throughout the country were extra vigilant.

For some exceedingly bizarre purpose, a person or persons unknown stuffed a kitten and some pieces of fried chicken into a two-foot-square box filled with old newspapers and then sealed it. A note which said only 'To Suzy' was attached to the box, and the package was left outside a government building in a major southern city.

At around six a.m., Sheriff Charles Herbert received a report from two patrolling deputies that they had spotted a mysterious box in the driveway between the county courthouse and the jail.

'It's right in the middle of the courthouse's loop driveway,' one of the officers told him. 'It could be a bomb that a terrorist has left to go off during business hours.'

Local police roped off the area, and a bomb squad was summoned from a nearby Army base. Sheriff Herbert was told to evacuate the jail, but he had no idea where he could put 400 inmates in a matter of minutes.

The Army bomb squad could detect no sound issuing from the box, so they made a decision to blow the top off the package.

Within moments, the air was filled with shredded newspapers and bits of fried chicken.

'Seconds later,' Deputy Sheriff Mark Pickett says, 'all of us onlookers were startled to hear the sounds of frightened mewing coming from the smoking box. Then, before our stunned eyes, a badly injured kitten started to crawl out of the box. It looked around at us, shook its head as if to shake out echoes of the explosion, then limped beneath a nearby car.'

Deputy Pickett retrieved the mutilated kitten from under the automobile and immediately decided to adopt him. 'The name Thunderball seemed very appropriate,' he says.

Vet Dr Cathy Seale removed Thunderball's left rear leg and treated his mutilated tail and lungs. 'It was a miracle that Thunderball was still basically in one place,' she says. 'With a resilience that is common among cats, I could see that he would pull through.'

Deputy Pickett says that Thunderball was an exceptionally sweet kitten. 'You'd think that he might be full of mistrust and anger towards humans after what happened to him, but he plays happily with me, my wife and our two other cats.'

'Thunderball was the innocent victim of the Iraqi terrorism scare that swept our country during the Persian Gulf conflict,' says Sheriff Herbert. 'We feared we might have a bomb in the box, but all we had was a harmless little kitten and some pieces of fried chicken.'

RONALD'S CAR RIDE FROM HELL

On the morning of 17 July, 1992, Estelle Littmann, of Montgomery, Alabama, was in her station wagon on her way to the bank where she had worked as a teller for over eleven years. She was only a few miles from her home when she was startled by a man in a brownish-coloured van who pulled up beside her and began to shout and wave wildly.

'I was frightened,' Mrs Littmann says. 'You hear all the time about killers and maniacs trying to assault women on the highways. At first I tried to ignore him.'

But the man in the van overtook her, flashed his signal lights and motioned for her to pull over.

'I thought, no way am I going to pull over and become the next victim of some serial killer. I floored the accelerator and shot around him at top speed. I was, in fact, driving about fifteen miles over the speed limit hoping that some cop would spot me on his radar and come to arrest me, and save me.'

When her persistent pursuer caught up to her once again, Estelle had another thought. Perhaps this was all connected to her position with the bank. She remembered seeing a movie or a television special about some bank robbers who first kidnapped certain members of a bank's personnel and then forced them to assist in the theft.

At last she spotted a housing development where a security guard was stationed. She felt certain that if she drove up to the guard on duty, the wacko nutcase following her would surely leave her alone.

As she pulled into the driveway of the guard's station, the man in the brown van honked his horn several times and drove on.

'I thought the pervert had to give me one last beep on his horn,' Mrs Littmann says, 'but I didn't care if he thought he was insulting me or not. At last, I was rid of him.'

The security guard stepped out of his station to enquire of her business, and she watched his face turn pale.

'Ma'am,' he blurted out, 'you got a cat on the top of your car!'

Estelle Littmann quickly unbuckled her seat belt and pushed open the door of the station wagon. Her mouth dropped open, and she knew that she became several shades paler than the security guard.

'There, on top of my station wagon, spread-eagled on the roof and clutching on the luggage rack for dear life was my black-and-white tom-cat, Ronald! The poor baby had just had a ride from hell, and he looked like he was frozen solid in complete and total fear.'

Mrs Littmann says that it took two or three days of lots of tender loving care to 'unthaw' Ronald, but he was soon doing fine, none the worse for his ride of terror on the top of a speeding car.

THE PUSSY-CAT 'FROZEN WITH FEAR' WAS REALLY A GARGOYLE MADE OF STONE

Although the following story may sound like a madcap Monty Python comedy sketch, a tipsy cat lover in Brighton fell thirty feet from an office building when he tried to rescue a kitty that was actually a stone gargoyle.

The young man was out with friends celebrating his twenty-third birthday when he spotted what he believed was a frightened cat clinging to the outside of a three-storey building.

'There's no question about it,' he said valiantly, 'duty calls. I must scale the wall, and I must rescue that poor, trembling, terrified cat.'

'I should think that there's a bit of risk involved,' one of his friends said, seeking to dissuade him. 'The poor thing looks awfully high up. Perhaps we should call the fire brigade or the RSPCA or some such professional cat rescuers.'

'The dangers inherent in climbing to a great height is certainly no reason to shirk one's responsibility to humane and noble deeds,' the stewed-to-the-gills Galahad decreed.

'If I am seeing what you are seeing,' another friend commented, squinting up at what appeared to be a feline form hugging the building for dear life, 'that is not a real cat, but a stone gargoyle. You know, the ugly creatures they put on buildings to frighten away evil spirits and all that sort of rubbish.'

'You've had far too much to drink,' the birthday celebrant scolded his pal. 'Imagine mistaking a poor frightened pussy-cat for a wretched gargoyle on Notre-Dame Cathedral or something. You should go home if you're going to carry on like this.'

Shaking himself free of the restraining hands of two other friends, the tipsy rescuer began to climb the side of the building, carefully wedging desperate fingers and shaking shoe soles into every available crack and edge between the bricks and stones.

'I am going to rescue that cat,' he announced to the world in general and to his fellow celebrants in particular. 'I shall be its hero. My name shall be honoured among cat lovers throughout the world.'

But before the highly inebriated cat fancier could reach the life-like sculpture with the feline-like features, he lost his grip and fell thirty feet to the pavement. Several rounds of alcoholic birthday libations were unable to serve as any protective shield for his physical person, and he fractured his skull in the process.

Later, police authorities commented that the would-be rescuer, who was recovering in hospital, had said that he was convinced that the stone cat wasn't moving because it had been 'frozen with fear'. He was now willing to concede, however, that it must have been a stone gargoyle, content to remain on constant vigil against demons attacking the building, not a real-life, flesh-and-blood feline in distress.

SMOKEY ENDURED THIRTY-SEVEN DAYS IN AN EMPTY VENDING MACHINE

Laura Dalfonso had only had her smoky-grey Siamese for a little over a year when he disappeared in July 1990.

'I was heartbroken,' she says. 'I own a vending machine business in a suburb of Baton Rouge, Louisiana – and I had got into the routine of taking Smokey everywhere with me on my rounds. He sat on a pillow next to my chair when we watched television, and he rode on my lap whenever we went anywhere in the car.'

Laura spent the days after Smokey disappeared searching the neighbourhood and tacking up reward posters for his return in all the malls and supermarkets.

'I got to thinking that I had sold six vending machines to Martin Napier the day that Smokey disappeared,' Laura says, 'and I started getting a feeling that Smokey might have somehow got inside one of those machines.'

Napier was sympathetic to Laura's loss when she called him on the phone. He promised to go out to his warehouse and check the machines straight away.

'I did check them out just as I promised,' Napier says. 'But I didn't open them up and look inside. After all, every slot and opening was closed, so I couldn't see any way on earth a cat could have wriggled between a hairline crack and got inside. Besides, I put my ear to every one of those machines to listen for anything that sounded like a cat, and there were no strange sounds coming from any of them.'

Laura continued her lonely quest, taping up hundreds of 'lost cat' signs and walking through the woods and nearby neighbourhoods calling Smokey's name. After thirty days, she gave up hope that she would ever see Smokey again.

At the same time, Martin Napier was beginning to prepare the vending machines for service. A local school board had purchased all six of them, and it was nearly time to install the machines for the autumn term.

'You could have knocked me over with a feather when I

opened up the fourth machine and saw these big blue eyes looking up at me from a scruffy cat face,' Napier says. 'It was Laura's cat Smokey all right. Somehow he had managed to get himself hidden away in a compartment that was nineteen by thirty inches – and only eight inches high.'

Napier put his hand out, and Smokey rubbed his head against the man's palm.

'It was obvious that the cat was just too weak even to stand up. I rushed him to a veterinarian, who told me that Smokey had probably lost about half his weight through dehydration and malnutrition.'

Dr Carla Rhea admitted that thirty-seven days without food or water was an amazing feat of endurance, but she added that cats seem to have the ability to go for long periods without nourishment of any kind.

When he was certain that Smokey would be all right, Martin Napier called Laura and gave her the good news. She had been right about Smokey having been in one of the machines, he told her, '. . . but he's going to be all right, even after thirty-seven days of solitary confinement – without bread and water.'

Smokey made a full recovery, and he returned to Laura to go everywhere by her side once again.

CHAPTER FIVE

MEAN AND SCARY CATS

In his book *Possession and Exorcism*, Hans Naegeli-Osjord relates an account of a cat which he suggests might well have been possessed by a demonic entity. According to Naegeli-Osjord, he was given the account in a personal conversation with Dr Vintila Horia of Madrid.

In Romania, his country of origin, Dr Horia claimed to have known a lady who owned a cat that urinated on every religious book, even if they should be lying underneath other non-religious texts.

'Once,' reported Dr Horia, 'the lady wanted to hang up [a religious] icon but hammered the nail in crooked. She put the icon on the table and, while looking for a new nail, left the room for a short moment. In her absence, the cat jumped on the table and pawed the icon until it fell and was badly damaged.'

The ostensibly anti-religious feline also behaved strangely in other ways and, according to its owner, was once squarely run over by a car without suffering any injuries.

Fully believing that possession is a 'unique phenomenon' that is not to be confused with such ego-splitting psychological maladies as clinical schizophrenia, Naegeli-Osjord maintains that even animals may be 'infiltrated by the demonic in some way'.

While cats tend to be solitary creatures, the author notes, they do have close relationships with 'significant contact persons'. In the bizarre case referred to above, 'the demonic . . . may have transferred into the cat' through an association with a possessed human.

The centuries-old ecclesiastical debate about whether or

not demonic possession exists – and, as in the case above, whether or not it can be transferred to animals in general and cats in particular – is not within the province of this book. There are weird cases, however, where logical explanations simply do not exist to rationalize a cat's extremely violent behaviour patterns or a cat's singular persecution of a particular individual.

SHEILA'S RAMPAGE OF TERROR

To Andrew and Klara Faber, Sheila, their female grey and white Scottish Fold, was the model of feline propriety and gentleness. They were astonished in March 1990 to discover that their neighbours in a suburb of Grand Rapids, Michigan, were about to launch a lawsuit against them.

'We knew that Sheila tended to roam while Andy and I were at work,' Klara admits, 'but we had no idea of the kind of mischief that she was allegedly getting into with our neighbours.'

The Fabers' neighbours regarded Sheila's activities as having stretched far beyond the boundaries of 'mischief'. It seemed to them the cat was purposefully conducting some kind of evil vendetta against them.

Henry Gonshak stated that Sheila not only dug up their plants and vegetables almost as fast as he and his wife Jean could plant them, the ornery cat also invaded their home.

'We would return from work or shopping and find that our sofa pillows had been ripped to shreds,' he says. 'Our indoor plants would be spilled on the carpet, and it was disgustingly obvious that a cat had used some of the soil for a makeshift litter box. And sometimes it didn't bother with the soil. It left its faeces on a sofa cushion.'

The Gonshaks did confront the Fabers at that time, and they were troubled that Sheila's owners did not seem to take them seriously.

'Andrew and Klara tried to convince us that we were

mistaken,' Jean Gonshak says. 'It just couldn't be their precious Sheila doing such terrible things. It had to be another cat.'

But on the very next day, the Gonshaks returned to find several valuable plates lying smashed on the dining-room floor. 'A number of Jean's most valuable collector plates had been dislodged from their places on the wall, and they had been dashed to the floor. We knew that Sheila had paid our home another visit.'

Jean remembered the time that Sheila had ruined a family gathering at Christmas time.

'We had invited our children and their families to join us first at church on Christmas morning, then come back to the house for a holiday meal. We found Sheila in our kitchen, contentedly dining on the turkey. Mashed potatoes and pumpkin pies had been splattered all over the floor.'

Harry Gonshak said that he would happily have rent Sheila limb from limb on that occasion, but the cat seemed literally to disappear before their eyes.

'I don't know how the fiend managed it, but it somehow left the kitchen and got away from us. I went right to the telephone and called the Society for the Prevention of Cruelty to Animals to come and pick up the damned cat; but it being Christmas and all, there was no one to come out to the neighbourhood that day.'

Neighbours Leonard and Ellie Murillo also had their complaint to file against the Fabers and Sheila, the monster cat.

'Ellie is extremely allergic to cats,' Mr Murillo says. 'And while we like cats, we could never have one for a pet because of her allergy. We could never have one in the house.

'We could not understand it,' he continued. 'when one night, around three in the morning, I had to rush Ellie to the emergency section of the hospital because she could not breathe. It was weird, because I suffer from asthma and I was having great difficulty breathing as well.'

The next afternoon, when Leonard and Ellie returned to their home and were well enough to investigate the mysterious onset of their allergy and asthma attack, they found cat hairs on Ellie's pillow.

'We looked under the bed and saw balls of white and grey cat fur. We knew that the Fabers' cat Sheila had somehow invaded our home.'

Leonard and Ellie began to make it a habit to check their pillows and sheets carefully before retiring. After discovering clumps of cat hair on their pillows and under the bed for three nights in a row, the Murillos followed through on a call to the SPCA.

The fur flew between them and the Fabers when an officer arrived to apprehend Sheila and take her into temporary custody, but they angrily stood their ground and informed the Fabers in no uncertain terms that they would not tolerate any more uninvited visits from the cat.

'I paid the fine,' Andrew Faber says, 'but I wanted to know why Leonard and Ellie had done such a thing as to turn Sheila in to the SPCA. When they told me about their allergy and asthma attacks and the cat hairs on their bed, I just couldn't believe that our cat could possibly be responsible for such a thing. It seemed ridiculous.

'I asked them how Sheila could have got into their locked house and why she would leave her hair all over and under their bed. I thought they were becoming hysterical when they claimed that Sheila had done it deliberately to make them ill. They actually said that they thought our cat was evil.'

When the Fabers got word that the Gonshaks were about to file a $50,000 lawsuit against them because of Sheila's hellish raids on their home, Andrew decided to ask a farmer friend of his to take the cat to the country for a while until things in the neighbourhood cooled down.

Andrew's friend returned Sheila after ten days. 'Your cat is a monster, pal,' he complained. 'She tore hell out of my cats, nearly blinded our German shepherd, and killed three of our chickens. When we tried to keep her in the house and away from the other farm animals, she ripped our best sofa to shreds.'

All this was so hard to believe as Klara held the purring and seemingly gentle Sheila in her arms.

The lawsuit never came to court, but a judge did order Andrew and Klara to keep their cat indoors or on a leash.

'We agreed to settle with the Gonshaks' insurance companies, because we really do wish to keep peace with our neighbours,' Klara Faber says.

'These days Sheila stays under lock and key in the house or on a thirty-foot leash when she is outside. It is just so hard to imagine that our sweet little Sheila really was responsible for all those terrible things that our neighbours claim.'

While Sheila may be an angel to Andrew and Klara, she will always be a demon in the opinion of the Murillos and the Gonshaks.

DEVIL CAT KILLS WOMAN AFTER STALKING HER FOR THREE YEARS

On 24 July 1989, Mrs Alicia Ontiveros, aged eighty-two, of Santa Monica, California, was killed by a savage black tom-cat that had stalked her for over three years.

'It was all so absolutely weird and terrible,' her daughter Susana Ferrucci says. 'It was as if Mom was living in a real-life horror movie. For three years she was stalked wherever she went by this big black tom-cat. None of us could ever figure out why this cat had it in for her. None of us could ever find out where it had come from.'

Mrs Ontiveros' brother Robert said that his sister had asked him whether or not the family might have had some curse placed on it.

'This cat came from nowhere to attack me and make my life miserable,' she said to him. 'It has clawed me and bitten me time after time. Why me?'

Robert said that he could not provide his sister with a satisfactory answer to this most bizarre of situations.

'Has someone placed a curse on me?' she asked him on

more than one occasion. 'Or was there some horrible act done to a cat by our family in generations past for which fate has decreed that I must pay?'

Robert could only attempt to assure her that he had no knowledge of such supernatural circumstances. 'Even in the old country where our people were ranchers and farmers, I have never heard of any of our family mistreating or abusing cats or any other kind of animal.'

Her son, Arman Ontiveros, confessed that he had doubted his mother's story when the stalking first began in December of 1985.

'I thought, well, Mom is getting on in years. She has begun to imagine strange things about some stray cat she sees every now and then. And since she said the cat was black, well, you know, I figured it was just some old superstition.

'I made an awful mistake,' Arman continues, expressing his guilt and his grief. 'I should have listened to my mother. I should not have judged her as being hysterical. Most of all, I should have killed that damn cat!'

Alicia Ontiveros was walking with her next-door neighbour, seventy-four-year-old Nancy Goodwine, when the first attack occurred.

'We were on our way to a nearby market to buy some groceries,' Mrs Goodwine says. 'We always tried to walk together to the grocery store. Anyway, we had hardly walked half a block when this big black cat came flying out of the bushes and landed on Alicia's right arm.

'Alicia and I both screamed in absolute horror. I could tell that Alicia was in awful pain. I hit at the cat with my purse, and Alicia swung her arm back and forth trying to free herself from the cat's claws and teeth.

'We finally got Alicia away from the monster, but it had left long, deep, bleeding grooves all down the side of her arm. We went back into her house and called a taxi, and I went with her to the doctor to get her bandaged and get her some shots against infection.'

From that day on, Alicia Ontiveros became the constant prey of a relentless hunter. It was impossible for her to set one step outside her home without the vicious black cat appearing from somewhere – from behind a bush, from the darkening shadows, from her own front steps – to scratch and claw at her body.

'How can it always be there whenever I want to leave my home?' she asked her friends and neighbours. 'Does it ever eat or sleep? Does it ever do anything other than lie in wait for me?'

The savage tom-cat was not always content merely to lie in wait for Mrs Ontiveros' emergence from her house. On occasions, it tried to claw open a door or a window.

'One afternoon, when we were having coffee in her kitchen, we heard this terrible growling noise,' Mrs Goodwine recalls. 'We both jumped to our feet, and were horrified to see the big black cat trying to squeeze itself through this small opening between the window and the sill.

'I grabbed a broom and beat at its head until it withdrew. I was afraid then that the devil cat would begin stalking me, but it never did. It just kept after Alicia.'

From that day on, Alicia Ontiveros literally became a prisoner in her own home. She kept the doors and windows closed and locked even in the hottest weather, and she began to order her groceries over the telephone.

One evening, nearly two years after the nightmare had begun, Mrs Ontiveros told her daughter Susana that she had come to believe the cat to be Satan who was tormenting her in feline form.

'I tried to reason with her,' Susana says, 'but she had it all worked out in her own mind.'

Alicia Ontiveros could present a convincing argument that the black cat was a demonic entity.

'Why,' she would ask, 'would a cat suddenly appear from nowhere to persecute me? How can it always know the exact time I wish to leave my home? What ordinary cat would continue to stalk me for such a long period of time? Yes, it is true. Satan waits for me outside my door.'

On many occasions, Robert Ontiveros tried to catch the feline fiend that was so rigorously tormenting his sister.

'Whenever I came round to put an end to his persecution of Alicia, the beast would be nowhere in sight,' he says. 'Yet if she attempted to venture out after I had telephoned from the corner that all was clear, the demon would come spitting, hissing and scratching at her, seemingly from out of nowhere.'

On 22 July 1989, Alicia Ontiveros received word that her dear friend Jeanne Lebeau had died. The funeral service, she was told, would be held on 24 July.

'I will attend Jeanne's funeral in spite of the devil cat,' she told Mrs Goodwine. 'The church is only two blocks away, and nothing can stop me from walking there to pay my last respects to a dear old friend.'

On 24 July, at two o'clock in the afternoon, Alicia Ontiveros opened the door to face her dark nemesis. The scenario the investigating police officers reconstructed went something like this:

The large black tom-cat was sitting on the step, his angry green eyes riveted on the elderly woman. Then, incredibly, the shrieking bundle of fury leaped on to her chest, dug its claws firmly into her flesh, and savagely tore her throat open with its fangs.

Mrs Ontiveros staggered back inside her home, and in a few minutes the life force had spurted out of her.

'We found blood on the steps, on the door, and sprayed throughout the house,' a police officer said. 'There was blood on the furniture, through the kitchen and hallway . . . on the carpets and walls.'

Mourning the loss of her friend and shuddering over the horrible nature of her death, Mrs Goodwine was critical of Mrs Ontiveros' son.

'Arman should have taken his mother seriously when she first told him about that devil cat,' she says. 'He should have sat outside her house and waited and waited until he had captured that demon from hell.'

According to the police report, a large black tom-cat was snared by an animal control officer in the area. It seemed likely that it was the same cat that had terrorized and stalked

Mrs Ontiveros for three years. It was soon destroyed on the judgement that it was the killer cat.

'There are a lot of black cats in the world,' Mrs Goodwine comments wryly. 'Let us hope they destroyed the right one. I would hate to think that spawn of Satan is somewhere out there stalking another elderly victim.'

CAT FROM HELL TERRORIZES OREGON FAMILY

'I keep having this terrible nightmare,' Becky MacDaniels says. 'I hear the doorbell ring, and when I open the door, that godawful cat from hell is standing there smiling up at me. "Hi, there," it says. "I'm back! Want some more?"'

Becky and her two teenage sons, Hugh and Terry, were working in their Washington, Oregon, garden on a peaceful Saturday afternoon in September 1992 when they were attacked by a ferocious stray cat.

'The fiend came at us from out of nowhere,' Becky says. 'This strange white cat just came bounding at us and started attacking us. Our three dogs were shut up in the house or they might have been able to drive it off. If my husband Lance had been home, he probably would have shot the demon and we would have been done with it.'

As it was, the devilish cat clawed at their hands and whatever body parts presented themselves within its range. Then, hissing and spitting, the vicious creature withdrew to a tree branch.

'But it wasn't retreating,' Becky says. 'It just wanted a perch from where it could dive on us.'

Like a maddened Valkyrie swinging her sword and dagger, the cat pounced on Hugh's back and slashed at him with both front paws. Then, while the older boy reeled in pain, the fiend leaped to his younger brother's back and began chewing at his neck.

'By now, I figured the diabolical thing has got to have

rabies and has gone berserk,' Becky says. 'All I can see is that it is chewing on Terry's neck, and I reached out for it with both hands, intending to rip it off and toss it as far as I could. Well, it latched on to me like a chainsaw and started ripping my hands and fingers to bloody shreds.'

At last the beleagured MacDaniels family managed to escape the infernal cat's vicious onslaughts and get inside their house.

They called the police, and a few hours later Chief Gordon Simansen had captured the ferocious feline in a skunk trap.

'It was without a doubt the meanest cat that I had ever seen,' Chief Simansen says. 'It snarled at you like a caged panther, and it would try to get at you right through the wires of the cage.'

The cat, nicknamed the Terminator by the Chief and his men, was taken to the pound for a ten-day rabies observation period.

'If the thing had rabies, then the MacDaniels family would have been in for more grief, for they would have had to undergo a painful vaccination process,' Chief Simansen says.

As incredible as it may seem, after two days the fiendish cat escaped from the pound – and somehow managed to find its way back to the MacDaniels' home.

Becky had just returned from the hospital where she had been receiving treatment for her chewed and mangled hands.

'I had barely walked in the door,' she says. 'I mean, that damned diabolical cat almost beat me home. I could not believe it when that fiend out of hell came running at me in my own kitchen. That cat was just plain crazy. It started jumping at the walls, tearing off the wallpaper. How do you figure that?

'Hugh set our three dogs after it, and she took them all on and nailed them one by one. Two black Labs and a beagle, and she had them all yelping and running for cover.

'After the dogs cleared out, so did the boys and I. Over my shoulder, I could see the cat from hell going to work on our sofa and stuffed chairs. The kids and I just got the blazes out of the house.'

Becky and her sons watched the cat 'making a total wreck' of their living room, and then, strangely enough, the animal began to wind down, as if its bizarre vendetta against the MacDaniels family had somehow been satisfied – at least momentarily.

Hugh took advantage of the cat's sudden period of calm to lure it into an old cage that had once housed a pet rabbit. Terry called Police Chief Simansen with the outlandish news that the cat from hell had once again returned to terrorize them.

'This whole incident is one of the weirdest I have ever dealt with in my twenty-five-year career as a law enforcement officer,' Chief Simansen says. 'My men and I could hardly believe that the ornery cat had escaped and found its way back to the MacDaniels' home. It really seemed as if that stray cat felt that it had some evil mission to hurt them and to trash their home.'

'Thank heavens our would-be assassin did not have rabies,' Becky MacDaniels says. 'The report came back from the laboratory negative.'

Within a few days, the feline terrorist was destroyed in the pound, its devilish spirit freed to return to whatever nightmare from which it had escaped.

COME FRY WITH ME

For six years Portia the Parrot and Bunta the Burmese cat had been conducting a running feud that, in retrospect, Scott and Joan Linttelman of Douglas, Nebraska, admit they should have guessed would end in disaster for one of the combatants.

'Portia was my birthday present in 1986,' Joan says, 'and cat and bird took an instant dislike to one another. We had already had Bunta for three years, so I guess he felt that he had earned the monopoly on our affections.

'Bunta would stand under Portia's cage and hiss up at her,

and Portia would begin the most horrendous squawking whenever she spotted him coming near.'

On one occasion, Bunta knocked the cage stand off-balance and sent Portia – seeds, water dish, toy bell and all – crashing to the floor.

'It was a good thing we were home or I'm certain that Bunta would have killed Portia at that time,' Joan says.

It was also on the occasion of Portia's near-death experience that Joan and Scott soundly scolded Bunta with the shaming accusation of 'Bad cat! Bad, bad cat! Bad, bad Bunta!'

Portia's keen ear for mimicry immediately recorded the litany of 'bad, bad cat . . . bad, bad Bunta' in an almost perfect recreation of Joan's voice.

The feud continued within hissing and squawking perimeters until that fateful evening in April 1992.

'For whatever reason, Portia was really on Bunta's case that night,' Scott says. 'She squawked "bad, bad Bunta" over and over until it was getting on everyone's nerves.

'It finally got to the point where Bunta couldn't handle it, and he was in the process of toppling the cage when I walked into the room and rescued Portia from a nasty fall.'

Because he was in the midst of a household chore and didn't have a great deal of time to settle the eternal feud between bird and cat, Scott glanced quickly about and sighted what, with a fleeting assessment of the household environment, he thought would be a safer spot to place the parrot's cage.

'The top of the stove seemed to me to be a safe place of retreat for Portia the bigmouth, so I removed the cage from its stand, set it atop the kitchen stove, and went about my work. By the time I finished my task at hand it was bedtime and I retired without giving Portia and Bunta another thought.'

Imbued with a renewed sense of security on the stove where she knew the cat could not reach her, Portia had once again begun the monotonous chant that reminded Bunta of his less than perfect state of existence. 'Bad, bad cat! Bad, bad Bunta!' sounded over and over again from the beak of the smug parrot.

At last, after several hours of such railing, Bunta could take no more. Angrily he jumped up on the counter next to the stove and knocked over a coffee pot – which fell against a switch that turned on the burner under Portia's plastic-bottomed cage.

Whether one interprets such a bizarre domino effect of cat to pot to switch to burner as pure coincidence or as Bunta's response to the instructions of an evil intelligence outside himself will probably depend upon one's individual cosmology. However, the burning fact remains that within minutes Joan Linttelman's $500 West African parrot had been fried to a crisp.

'We had already gone to bed for the night,' Scott says, 'but were awakened by the smell of the acrid smoke that was filling the house. We rushed into the kitchen and saw that Portia was history and that the fire had begun to spread to the counter. We dialled 911 and got out of the house fast . . . and so did Bunta!'

'I guess Bunta just couldn't take Portia's squawking any longer,' Joan says. 'I just wish that she hadn't had to die such a terrible death.'

At last report, Bunta seems to be a much happier cat – smug, one might say.

STRANGE MONSTER CATS THAT HAUNT THE UNITED STATES

On Monday evening, 21 August 1978, Mrs Evelyn Cayton of Belleville, Ohio, along with some friends, was standing on her front porch. Suddenly, everyone present heard heard strange noises coming from the direction of a demolished chicken coop that was located just to the right of the house. Mrs Cayton turned on her flashlight and two pairs of large yellow eyes were reflected in the light.

At the same time eighteen-year-old Scott Patterson drove his car towards the coop in the hope of getting a better look with his headlights at whatever was causing the disturbance. He most certainly accomplished his goal.

The yellow eyes belonged to what appeared to be two large, black cat-like creatures that lunged towards the headlights of his car. All the other witnesses fled into the house.

After the creatures had run off into the night, Patterson immediately telephoned the Stark County Sheriff's office, and several deputies were dispatched to check on the incident. Deputy Sheriff James Shannon reportedly smelled a strong, foul stench in the area of the old chicken coop, and he collected hair samples and made casts of some very strange-looking paw prints.

In the days and weeks that followed, other peculiar cat creatures and bizarre animal forms were sighted in the region, but all of the weird entities escaped from their pursuers completely unscathed.

Timothy Green Beckley, author of several books on the unknown, has pointed out that throughout the literature of the occult, strange and unusual animal entities have often been associated with demonology, Satanism and the sinister side of the Black Arts. Most of these hideous and perverse creatures assume a cat-like or a reptilian form.

'These cat-like beings that stalk our farms and backwoods do not seem to be flesh and blood in the sense that we consider other living things,' Beckley says. 'It seems as though it is impossible to trap them; and when they have been shot, they simply disappear in the twinkling of an eye – indicating that they may be more like ghosts than anything else.

'Perhaps there are these cat-like creatures that exist in other realms alongside us, who have always been more etheric in content than created of flesh and blood like our own beloved pets.'

*

Even now, as I write this chapter in November 1992, I am carefully reading the local newspapers for accounts of the mysterious black cats that have appeared in various parts of Iowa over the past fifty years or so. The frightening felines usually accomplish their first solid materializations shortly after the early snows have begun to bank over the shattered clumps of harvested cornstalks and the clods of recently ploughed earth.

Any day now, I am anticipating, some farmer will spot one of the creatures – stark and dark against the white drifts – crouching near his mailbox at the end of the lane. Or maybe the phantom cat will be bothering his chickens.

I remember clearly in the winter of 1971 when a strange cat-like creature was sighted in northeastern Iowa. Whatever the thing was, it proved itself to be equipped with an enormous appetite by eating large sections from several pigs. Perhaps in self-defence – or maybe just for sport – it broke the necks of a number of large dogs.

I will be disappointed if there aren't at least a few accounts of ghostly black felines in the approaching winter months. The monster cats have been haunting Iowans intermittently ever since I can remember; and now that my wife Sherry and I have just returned to Iowa after fifteen years in the deserts of Arizona, I will take it personally if they don't materialize in the winter of '92!

Year after year, in nearly every section of the United States, sensible men and women file reports of large, cat-like monsters marauding about the landscape. A really strange aspect of their raids on farms and ranches is that these cat creatures are never shot or killed – even though they are widely and earnestly hunted by experienced woodsmen.

And it is not because the weird beasties don't leave tracks, because they do. They leave cat-like paw prints all over the place – paw prints that can never be precisely identified, but which can be demonstrated beyond doubt to be not those of any known indigenous animal.

In 1968, a Connecticut Company bus driver swore that he had seen something that looked like a baby tiger or a huge tabby cat walk across Valley Street and disappear into the brush. He told police officers that he had made the sighting at about 5 p.m. near West Rock.

Although seven New Haven police cruisers were on the scene within minutes of the call, they could find no creature that resembled a monster cat in the area.

At about the sme time in Branford, Connecticut, a large, unidentified cat creature was seen near the drive of Senator Lucy T. Hammer's forty-acre country estate.

It had been the senator's husband who had first sighted the great cat-like animal strutting near their driveway. Thorvald Hammer, an iron company executive, had been eating breakfast when he spotted the bizarre intruder.

The tracking dogs of game wardens and police were able to find only the slashed remains of a squirrel.

Later, in her comments to journalists, Senator Hammer said that her husband had left the house and his breakfast and had watched the mysterious animal walking in a 'most stately manner down our path'. The iron company executive had lost sight of the creature when it went round a bend.

'The strange animal must have gone into the woods,' she concluded.

Or did the cat creature walk round the bend and re-enter the other dimension of time and space from which it had briefly emerged?

Whenever farmers and ranchers in Iowa, South Dakota, Nebraska or Ohio complain that a monstrous cat has been mangling their livestock, it is easy enough to theorize that a cougar has somehow migrated from a more western state in search of plentiful hunting grounds. The trouble is, none of the physical trace evidence ever fits that of a nomadic cougar, puma, mountain lion or panther (they're all different names for the same big cat, depending on which section of the country you hail from).

In May and June 1959 (to choose one of hundreds of reports), residents of the western section of Lorain County, Ohio, were having problems with a giant cat-like beast possessed of a large head, a huge, light-brown body, and an insatiable appetite for dogs, cats and sheep.

Mrs Iva Witteman, of Columbia Station in Lorain County, went out to check her eight sheep at about eight p.m. She found six of them literally ripped apart. One had been completely skinned, and another was missing.

A sheriff's deputy said that he had never seen anything like it, and he ruled out a dog pack as the wanton marauders. Mr and Mrs Witteman and a friend had been in their house, only 250 yards from the pasture in which the sheep were kept, and they had heard nothing.

In July 1964, the tales of cat creatures now featured a five-foot tall, tailless, earless, 200-pound feline that walked on its hind legs.

Two campers on Mt Tamalpais in Marin County, California, complained to authorities that two such entities had disturbed them on three different occasions. They reported that the cat people had heads close to their bodies and were very muscular below the shoulders. In one instance, the two campers had heard the creatures 'chittering' back and forth for about seven hours.

Samuel Johnson, a Chicago motorist, confronted his worst cat-monster nightmare on a road near Niles, Michigan. He could remember it only as 'something that had red eyes, brown hair, and squealed'. Johnson's car window had been shattered in four places where he said the creature had struck it.

On 10 April 1970, Mike Busby of Cairo, Illinois, was travelling on Route 3 to Olive Branch to pick up his wife. About a mile south of Olive Branch on the dark, deserted road that parallels the edge of Shawnee National Forest, Busby experienced car trouble. Grumbling his frustration, Busby got out of the car and popped open the bonnet.

Before he had time to glance at the motor he was distracted by a noise to his left. Without warning, an incredible cat-like form, about six feet tall, moved in on him and hit him in the face.

Busby and his monstrous attacker fell to the road, bound together in a desperate struggle. Dull claws ripped at his clothing, and Busby sought with all his strength to hold the thing's mouth open and at arm's length so its awful teeth could not tear his throat.

Although he was not able to identify clearly what it was that had seized him, Busby said later that he could feel something fuzzy around its mouth and that the thing's body hair was short and wiry, like steel wool.

The cat creature kept emitting deep, soft growls. 'Sounds unlike anything that I've ever heard,' Busby said.

After what must have seemed like an eternity locked in a death struggle, a diesel truck approached with bright headlights and the roar of a powerful motor – a combination of factors that appeared to frighten Busby's attacker back into the forest.

Spotlighted for a moment in the glare of the headlights, the creature appeared to be 'a sleek, shiny black colour'. Busby also noted that it ran away with heavy, thudding feet.

John Hartsworth, the truck driver with the fortuitous timing, stated that the thing that he had seen in the light from his headlamps looked like some kind of 'giant cat' until it had raised itself off Busby and run into the forest on its hind legs.

Just when we were about to conclude that we are being attacked by vicious alien cat creatures from the undiscovered planet Felix, who seek to do us nothing but harm, consider the following account.

When six-year-old Debbie Dierking disappeared from her home in northern Michigan at about six p.m. on 15 August 1988, local police officers, state police, a crew of volunteers and two police bloodhounds meticulously scoured a four-mile wooded area.

Understandably, the Dierking family was in shock. There was no ransom note, so kidnapping was thankfully ruled out. In point of fact, the police could not imagine how a middle-class family like the Dierkings could have been assessed by any professional criminal as being wealthy enough to pay ransom demands, but good police work required worrying about the wackos who might not be capable of correctly interpreting the family's modest neighbourhood and six-year-old Chevrolet in the driveway as an indicator of income.

It should go without saying that the Dierking household had been carefully searched before the original alarm concerning Debbie's absence had been issued. In addition, a Deputy Police Chief and the rector of the Roman Catholic church the Dierkings attended had also explored the house carefully three times.

Yet, incredible as it may seem, Debbie, the object of the masive search, was found before dawn the next morning, peacefully sleeping in her own bed.

When Debbie's parents, gratefully weeping yet stunned and incredulous, asked her where she had been, she stubbornly refused to tell them.

Stern police officers, solicitous neighbours, coaxing relatives all got the same answer: 'I'm not telling!'

Investigators wondered if some kidnapper had decided better of what could prove to be a dangerous and unprofitable gambit and had returned the child, desperately making a game of all of it in Debbie's mind and eliciting a promise from her that she would not tell where or with whom she had been.

Several days later, though, the girl at last confided in her mother that she had been found in the forest and safely returned to her bed by a 'cat guy', who looked like 'the nice lion man' on the *Beauty and the Beast* television show. 'You know,' she smiled and crinkled her nose, 'the nice cat man with the cape who lives in the sewer and saves the pretty lady.'

If Debbie's account can be believed, then some cat-like entity – or some person wearing cat-creature make-up similar to that donned by actor Ron Perlman in the television series – rescued her and escorted her safely back home.

Is it possible that some cosmic, interdimensional being with cat-like features and feline appearance removed the child for a time for some unfathomable purpose of his own, then brought her back to the physical plane of reality, making her first promise not to betray his secret?

If there is another, unknown dimension somehow sharing this planet with our own three-dimensional borders of reality, it may be safe to assume that it is inhabited by an intelligent species of some kind who share their world with assorted animals, birds, reptiles, fish and so forth. And if it is possible that from time to time there appear 'holes' or 'doorways' in our dimension and theirs, which permit passage between the two worlds, then it may be that all the creatures of our legends, myths and nightmares have their origins on this other plane of reality.

THE BIZARRE MONSTER CATS OF GREAT BRITAIN

Strange monster cats have also been sighted from time to time in the British Isles – which constitutes an even greater enigma than the mysterious cat creatures of North America for there have never been any indigenous large cats in Great Britain. Both North and South America provide natural habitats for creatures such as pumas, jaguars and bobcats, but Britain has never harboured any known cats larger than plump, milk-fed tabbies.

According to local accounts, a creature that left cat-like tracks prowled Ireland for a four-month period in 1874 and killed as many as thirty sheep in a single night.

In March 1906, fifty-one sheep were slain in one evening near Guildford. It was soon after such a night of carnage that a woman walking in a field swore that she had been grabbed by a 'panther'.

In October 1925, according to the London *Daily Express*, a cat-like monster 'black in colour and of enormous size' had people in the district of Edale, Derbyshire, so frightened that they refused to leave their homes after dark. The huge cat creature left the carcasses of sheep scattered about 'with legs, shoulders and heads torn off; broken backs and pieces of flesh ripped off'.

In the autumn of 1962 reports were being circulated of a cat-like beast near the Heathy Park Reservoir in Hampshire. In August and September, several people reported having observed something that looked like a young lion. Such sightings of an unusual animal continued until the end of the year.

On 18 July 1963, at Oxleas Wood, Shooters Hill, in London, a lorry driver stated that shortly before dawn he had observed what he believed to be a leopard running across the road and into the park.

Later that same day, four policemen reported that a large, peculiar cat-like animal had leaped over the bonnet of their squad car and run into the woods. A subsequent search conducted by 126 police officers, 30 soldiers and 21 dogs failed to produce anything more substantial than large cat-like footprints.

After a gap of about a month, startled observers once again reported seeing a 'wild cat' in Heathy Park in September and October of 1963.

On 14 February 1964, things got much livelier when area residents told of having sighted a 'huge' cat-like monster. Massive claws that left prints two inches deep in the firm winter ground remained as physical evidence of the mysterious marauder.

At about the same time, the good folk of Norfolk were being shaken by close encounters with a beast that eye-witnesses insisted was a tiger . . . or perhaps a panther . . . or maybe a cheetah.

In September 1964, a rash of cat-creature sightings was reported in Surrey, with similar accounts also issuing from neighbouring Sussex, Hampshire and Berkshire. A certain consensus of details yielded a description of a giant, gold-coloured cat with a very long tail.

A woman in West Sussex, who confronted the beast while walking her dogs in the woods, said that it had to have been a puma, six feet long and three feet high by her hurried estimation. When her dogs pursued it into the woods, it emitted 'spitting and screeching sounds'.

Although the large cat easily out-distanced the pursuing canines, it did leave behind prints with clearly defined impressions of claws.

By January 1965, the police had received so many reports of 'pumas' and 'panthers' in Surrey that they issued warnings to the public that such a misplaced animal might indeed be wintering somewhere on the 4000-acre Hurtwood Common.

On 3 February, a girl riding her bicycle near Ashurst in the New Forest was startled by a 'leopard' as large as a horse that glared at her with 'ferocious eyes'.

Sightings of the cat creature were reported in their hundreds throughout 1966.

On 1 September, a woman driving near Chiddingfold, Hampshire, stopped her Land-Rover and got out for a walk. While negotiating a thistle patch, she stepped on the tail of a 'puma' and experienced the horror of having the monster rear up on its hind legs and strike her in the face with both front paws. With a stouthearted action born of conditional reflex, the woman smacked the large cat in the face with the stick that she carried. When it ran up a tree, she raced for help – but the creature had made good its escape before she could return with the proper authorities.

In their book *Creatures of the Outer Edge* (Warner Books, 1978), Jerome Clark and Loren Coleman report that the number of cat-creature sightings diminished during the years of 1967 and 1968, 'but by the fall of 1969, Englishmen were seeing panthers, some black, some brown'.

In December 1970, a number of witnesses from Kent claimed to have seen a 'puma' kill four sheep near Dover.

In 1971, the sightings of cat-like creatures resumed throughout various parts of England. According to numerous British-based researchers of strange and extraordinary phenomena, the reports of bizarre cat creatures have continued unabated ever since.

BIZARRE SUPERSTITIONS AND BELIEFS ABOUT CATS

Perhaps no animal inspires such feelings of devotion and dedication on the part of some, and such feelings of animosity and abhorrence on the part of others, as the cat. Throughout history, cats have been regarded as gods by certain cultures and as demons by others. With such a centuries-old mystique swirling around the figure of the cat, it is no wonder that those silent little paws have left such heavy imprints in the collective psyches of those who love them, those who revere them, and those who fear them.

According to Jewish tradition, God had no hand in the making of cats. The first female and male couple were snorted from the nostrils of a lion as it was boarding Noah's Ark.

Throughout the European tradition, the black cat is the familiar companion of witches. The Inquisitors, with their awful instruments of torture, decreed all cats to be demons, and they condemned nearly as many cats to the stake as those unfortunates identified as witches.

It is because of this baseless old ecclesiastical judgement that the sighting of a black cat is said to be an omen of misfortune and bad luck. Another common notion is that unhappiness and personal tragedy will soon follow in the wake of the black cat that crosses one's path.

The great British novelist Charles Dickens, who was always fascinated by tales of the supernatural and the macabre, spoke in his later years of the stories that his nursemaid had told him which, as a boy, caused him nightmares and cold sweats. One of them was about the Black Cat, and in his *The Uncommercial Traveller* he remembered that the grim tale was about 'a weird and glowing-eyed supernatural Tom, who was reputed to prowl about the world by night, sucking the breath of infancy, and who was endowed with a special thirst (as I was given to understand) for mine.'

Of all the animals over which humans convince themselves that they hold dominion, the cat is the only one that looks us in the eye. Perhaps it is that steady glance that scorns subservience and assures us that the cat possesses magical powers which it can use for good or for evil.

Some people feel that the unwavering stare of the cat can instill terror, even death, in the beholder. Such an unreasoning and phobic response to cats is known as ailurophobia. Hitler had plans to dominate the world with his Third Reich, but the sight of a cat sent him trembling. Napoleon Bonaparte arrogantly snatched the crown of Holy Roman Emperor from the Pope and conquered nearly the whole of Europe, but when he spotted a cat in his palace he shouted for help.

Such dread of cats may be genetically transmitted, for when Joseph Bonaparte, King of Naples, visited Saratoga Springs in 1825 he complained that he sensed a cat's presence, then fainted. Although his hosts assured his majesty that no such animal was anywhere present, a persistent search revealed a kitten hiding in a sideboard.

Henry III of England was another personage of royal blood who would faint at the very sight of a cat.

In addition to the glance that can bring about feelings of terror, folklore also empowers the cats' eyes with the ability to see in the dark. Since most other creatures can see only in daylight, to be able to see at night reverses the natural order of things. Any being that can do this simply has to be sinister, ominous and satanic.

In the Middle Ages, the brain of a black cat was considered an essential ingredient in all powerful potions.

A very ancient superstition has it that spirits are able to assume the forms of black animals, particularly black cats. Such a tradition only enhanced the cat's reputation as a harbinger of ill fortune. At the same time, women who believed themselves to be witches sought cats for the very reason that they *might* be possessed by a spirit and could thereby serve effectively as their familiar and do their bidding.

An old black-letter book entitled *Beware the Cat!* (1584) issues a warning that black cats may be witches in disguise. If one should kill a black cat believing that he has killed the witch, the brutal act does not necessarily guarantee the elimination of the servant of the devil – for a witch can assume the body of a cat nine times.

During the terrible witchcraft trials of the Inquisition, heretics under torture confessed to kissing cats' buttocks and toads' mouths and cavorting with them in blasphemous ceremonies. Some poor wretches claimed that Satan first appeared to them in the form of a cat, for it was commonly held that cats were allied with Lucifer in the great rebellion against God. Lucifer, so the counter-gospel proclaimed, was the true creator, and one day he would lead all his followers back to Heaven to cast the usurper deity from the throne of glory.

It seems likely that the contemporary passion for cats began in ancient Egypt, where the first domesticated cats descended from a wild ancestor called *Felis libyca*. Not only did the Egyptians not fear the black cat, but, rather, they revered it. A cemetery harbouring the mummies of thousands of black cats was unearthed in Egypt, and a cargo of the mummified felines was sent to Great Britain.

The popular folk belief that a cat possesses nine lives can be traced back to the inhabitants of those ancient Nile cities. Bast (or Ubasti), the Cat-Mother, was associated with the benevolent aspect of Hathor, the Lioness, and was said to have nine lives. The peculiar attribute of Bast's nine instant incarnations came to be associated in the common mind with all cats.

The Egyptians revered cats and elevated them far beyond the role of domestic pet in which we have placed them today. To the Egyptians, the cat was transformed from mouse-catcher to supreme deity, the 'Sayer of Great Words'. The Egyptian word for cat was *Mau*, which is at once an imitation of the animal's call and the nearly universal cry for mother. Cats came to be worshipped with such intensity that the wanton killing of one was punishable by death.

Because the old Egyptians had a great fear of the dark, they observed with awe that the cat, a creature of the night, walked the shadowed streets with confidence. Carefully considering the import of the cat's midnight vigils, the ancient Egyptian wise ones decided that the cat was solely responsible for preventing the world from falling into eternal darkness.

At the same time, the cat's nocturnal excursions made it a symbol of sexuality and fertility. It seems quite likely that there were seductive sirens on the Nile using make-up to mimic the hypnotic eyes and facial markings of the cat long before Cleopatra worked her magic on Caesar and Antony.

Bubastis, a city in Lower Egypt, dedicated itself to the worship of the cat. Each year some 700,000 pilgrims would journey to the city in May to participate in the cat festival.

During the Persian invasion of 529 BC the Egyptians' idealization of the cat eventually proved to be their undoing. Knowing full well the obsession of the Egyptian people with the divinity of felines, Cambyses, King of the Persians, made a cat a part of the standard issue to each of his soldiers. The Nile dwellers led by King Psammeticus III laid down their spears and bows for fear of harming the cat that each soldier carried, and the Persians conquered the city of Pelasium without a drop of blood being shed.

*

The cat was also held sacred in ancient India. Sanskrit writings make numerous references to the influence of the cat upon humankind.

In Scandinavian countries, girls used to try their very best to be married on a Friday, Freya's day. Freya, often depicted being drawn in a chariot by two cats, is the cat-goddess of the Nordic people. If a young woman married on a sunny Friday, then it was known that she had taken good care of the family cats and that Freya would bless the union.

Throughout the centuries shamans, sages and wise ones have been convinced of the mystical powers of the cat, and they have openly consulted their feline familiars. In Great Britain, especially in the rural areas of Wales, Scotland and southwest England, children were told to spend time petting cats, because it was sincerely believed that some of the pusses' psychic abilities would rub off on them.

THE VOODOO PRIEST 'PUT PUSS' ON HIM

In the book *True Experiences in Exotic ESP* edited by Martin Ebon, Grace N. Isaacs contributed a chapter entitled 'Psychic Animals of the Caribbean' in which she describes how a modern-day practitioner of the dark arts set a familiar spirit in the form of a cat on a clergyman of the Christian cloth.

It seems that the Reverend Mr R., an Australian who resided in Jamaica, took a member of his congregation to task for continuing to visit the *obeah* man, the local voodoo priest. The fellow who had received such a firm verbal 'spanking' from the minister did not respond in a penitent manner at all. He went straight to the *obeah* man and repeated the minister's scolding word for word. The Voodoo priest definitely felt that the Australian interloper had overstepped the bounds of ecumenical tolerance, and he sent word to Reverend R. that he had put 'puss 'pon him'.

As might be expected, the orthodox clergyman was quite amused by the threat of a cat being set upon him. He informed the *obeah* man's messenger that never in his life had he ever been frightened by nonsensical threats and that puss or no puss he would continue to perform his clerical duties as he saw fit.

A short time after having so summarily dismissed the Voodoo priest's messenger, however, the Reverend R. was forced to observe that he seldom walked the streets of the village without a cat following at his heels.

According to Ms Isaacs, 'If he visited friends or a member of the congregation, a cat would jump on the arm of his chair. On the last occasion before the nuisance abated, he preached for a minister in another parish, and a cat found its way to the pulpit and perched itself on the spot where the minister would have placed his notes. It refused to be driven away, and the verger at last had to remove it bodily.'

FOUND: THE CHESHIRE CAT'S SMILE!

Literary scholars and Lewis Carroll enthusiasts alike have long pondered the origin of the author's inspiration for Wonderland's Cheshire Cat. From what source did he derive the bizarre feline that grinned at Alice until only its smile remained?

While most Carrollphiles have been willing to credit creative genius as the reservoir into which the author dipped his pen, others have been quick to suggest that the toothsome cat with the lingering smile was first glimpsed by Carroll while in a drug-induced dream.

In July 1992, however, Joel Birenbaum discovered the original Cheshire Cat lurking in the shadows at St Peter's

Church in Croft, Durham; and the long-standing mystery of where Lewis Carroll got the idea of a cat that disappeared leaving only a smile behind was solved at last.

One of thirty-five members of the Lewis Carroll Society visiting the church as part of a pilgrimage to various locations frequented by the revered author, Birenbaum observed a most curious phenomenon. As he knelt at the altar of St Peter's, he noticed the image of a cat that had been crudely carved in relief on a stone wall panel.

As he knelt lower, he was astonished to perceive that the lighting in the tenth-century chapel created the illusion that the cat disappeared – except for its smile.

'When you look at the image of the cat from the front, it looks just like an ordinary cat,' Birenbaum illustrated for his fellow Carroll enthusiasts. 'But when you go down on your knees and look up, you can see only the grin and not the cat.'

Carroll, whose real name was Charles Lutwidge Dodgson, moved with his family from Cheshire to Croft when he was a boy of eleven. It seems likely, as Birenbaum has suggested, that the lad became intrigued by the illusion of the disappearing cat as he knelt in the chapel of St Peter's Church. The peculiar effect apparently so delighted him that he used the lingering feline grin as an attribute of the Cheshire Cat many years later in his famous *Alice's Adventures in Wonderland*.

CHAPTER SIX

EERIE GHOST CATS

Josh McCarthy, an elderly blind man of Milwaukee, Wisconsin, was practically inconsolable when his beloved Burmese cat died of old age.

'Dad had lived with us for about eight years,' says Esther Kelly, his youngest daughter. 'Old Oscar had kept him company for so many years. Dad would sit for hours in his old rocking chair, stroking Oscar, and telling stories to the kids about his life on the railroad. I didn't figure Dad would last long after Oscar died.'

And then, one incredible afternoon, Josh summoned his daughter to his side.

'Dad was crying and smiling at the same time,' Mrs Kelly recalls. '"Listen! Listen!" he said. "Old Oscar has come back to me."'

Mrs Kelly bent her head towards his lap as her father indicated. 'Oscar had this funny, weird, raspy kind of purr,' she says. 'And I could hear that old cat's familiar purring.'

She stepped back and could see the indentation of a weight on her father's lap. 'Dad was stroking an invisible cat, and he was happy again. Some mean-spirited folks might say that Dad is crazy – lost his mind when his old cat died. But I have heard that ghost cat purr, and I believe that it is there on his lap once again.

'I guess that Oscar's return has proved to our whole family that love can open a big door between life and death.'

Dr T. J. Muckle of Kingston, Ontario, watched in amazement as the ghost of his beloved cat manifested before his eyes. The Canadian medical doctor was sitting in his living room in the afternoon when he saw the family tabby floating slowly across the room. The remarkable tale of the floating ghost cat is recounted in John Robert Colombo's book, *Mackenzie King's Ghost, Plus 49 Other Canadian Hautings*.

Continuing the account, Dr Muckle said, 'Our cat, Tom, walked past me in mid-air, and he seemed completely real and alive except that he was floating. I was absolutely shocked and baffled.

'Sadly, I found out later that our cat had been run over by a car miles away at that precise moment.

'A neighbour who witnessed the accident phoned. But, by then, our dead cat had already come over to say goodbye to us, and perhaps to let us know he still loved us.'

Timothy Green Beckley, of Inner Light Publishing Company in New York, recalls his acquaintance with a ghost cat, the spirit of a favourite pet who apparently survived physical death.

'When I was in my early teens, my family had a very frisky cat named Sweety who had silver-grey hair and beautiful green eyes. Sweety would hide in all sorts of places in the house and yard. Yet whenever she heard the tinkling of a little bell that we kept near her food and water dish, she would come running at full speed. It was a funny sight to see her trying to scamper across a newly waxed floor, her legs moving rapidly – but her furry body standing still due to the highly polished and slippery linoleum surface.'

Sweety lived to a ripe old age, Beckley remembers, and the family was heartbroken when their lively feline friend finally did pass away.

'Many years later,' he says, 'my father still lived in the same house. Since my sister and her family have a place of their own nearby, they were able to visit "Pops" more frequently than I was able to. On several occasions, my sister Bobbyjane swore that she saw Sweety run by her as if she were on his way to eat.'

Bobbyjane insisted that she saw the ghost of their favourite pet many times. 'In fact, I've almost tripped over Sweety,' she says. 'She just zips right through the kitchen and then disappears.'

Beckley says that his sister's testimony is not without verification. 'My nephew Brian has said that he has seen a cat on the stairs leading to my grandmother's apartment. Although he has tried to catch the animal many times, the cat vanishes before his eyes.'

Beckley points out that Brian is much too young to have seen Sweety in real life. 'The cat died many years before he was born. Yet Brian's description of the ghost cat with the same silver-grey hair and the beautiful green eyes is so similiar as to be nerve-rattling.'

Since Timothy Green Beckley's publishing company specializes in books about UFOs, ESP, ghosts, prophecy and magic, he is considered an authority on the strange and the bizarre and is a frequent guest on radio and television talk shows.

Tim recalls a time a few years back when he was appearing on *The Dennis Benson Show*, which was broadcast over WDVE Radio in Pittsburgh, and learned that his family home was not unique in its possession of a ghost cat.

Around 8 a.m. a listener telephoned with the following story:

'I've got this huge German shepherd who is very playful. He used to run all over the house chasing my pet alley cat, Alex.

'Recently Alex got hit by a car and died. When the cat didn't show up around the house any more, the German shepherd acted like he'd lost his best friend. He really had the blues.

'Then one day I heard two sets of paws running back and forth in the hallway. I looked out of my bedroom door, and three was my dog chasing *something* down the hall. A few feet in front of the German shepherd, I could see the dim outline of Alex – transparent, but still visible just the same.

'The cat went right through the wall, and my poor dog nearly killed himself because he wasn't able to stop soon enough.'

The listener concluded his account by stating that Alex the ghostly cat had shown up four or five times after that initial appearance. He added that the German shepherd seemed happy that he had his old friend back.

Mrs Sarah Devietro was terribly distressed when she heard the news about Bucky. In tears she told her husband Tony that the beloved cat that they had given to friends had been put down.

'We only gave Bucky up because we thought we were getting too old to care for him properly,' she told him.

'Cissie and Dave had to put Bucky to sleep because the rules of their new apartment house forbade them to keep pets. Why, oh why, did they not call us and ask us to take Bucky back?'

Tony was also very upset. They had both loved the tomcat, who had been nearly fifteen years old. They would gladly have accepted the return of their old feline friend.

According to the Devietros, they first heard the scratching at the bottom of their bedroom door about a week after they learned the sad news of Bucky's execution. The noises became so insistent and so loud that they were both awakened from deep sleep.

'By all the saints,' Sarah says, 'Tony and I saw our bedroom door swing open. We keep a little nightlight on, so we could clearly see that nothing visible had entered our room. The door had been opened by an unseen force.'

And then, to their astonishment and their delight, the elderly couple felt something jump up on to their bed – and they *felt* Bucky bouncing across the covers the way he had always moved in life. Tears came to their eyes as they clearly heard the sound of affectionate purring fill the room.

'People can call us old fools if they like,' Tony says, 'but we have a real ghost cat in our home. We know that it is Bucky, and he jumps up on our bed nearly every night.'

Sarah said that she could sometimes feel the invisible cat rubbing up against her legs. 'A couple times we even found cat hairs on the sofa pillow in the living room. That spot used to be Bucky's favourite to sneak up and take a nap.'

The most important thing that Bucky's ghostly return demonstrates to Sarah and Tony is that their cat did not blame them for his unceremonious death by vet's injection.

'His coming back lets us know that he still loves us,' Tony says, 'and that love between animals and humans can reach across the grave. Sarah and I will probably be ghosts ourselves one day soon. Bucky has gone on ahead to find a home for us.'

Music teacher Ruth Wharton, who resides in Southern California, once owned a white, part-Siamese cat named Snooky which she loved very much.

'Snooky used to sit outside the door to the house and wait for my music pupils to arrive for a lesson,' Ms Wharton says. 'By positioning himself right beside the door, he would be certain to be petted by each of the pupils before they entered.'

Ms Wharton states her firm conviction that Snooky was very psychic. 'He would play and miaow to unknown spirit cats that I could not see. Snooky could also tell when my husband would come down the street in his car. Wherever he might be, Snooky would come running as fast as he could to welcome my husband home.'

One day after his scheduled feeding time, Snooky did not return. Ms Wharton says that she searched everywhere, calling his name over and over again. 'But Snooky never came home again.'

One month from the day he disappeared, Snooky's ghostly image appeared in the tree outside Ms Wharton's window.

'I was in the middle of giving a piano lesson when suddenly the pupils turned towards the window – and there on a branch in the tree was Snooky. It really was my cat, and he went up on to the roof and began to miaow. I went out on to the patio with my pupils and called to him, but we never heard him again.'

On two other occasions, however, Snooky did return in a

similar manner to inform his owner that he was alive and well – but in a very different form. He was now in spirit.

'Such experiences have convinced me that no one ever dies,' Ms Wharton says, 'whether you are a human or an animal.'

GABRIEL'S PROTECTIVE GAZE CIRCUMVENTED DEATH

Twilight was just beginning to lengthen the shadows in the northern Minnesota forest that day in November 1967. Craig Russell was hiking back to his pick-up truck after a day of hunting when he sensed something stirring in the brush.

'I was disgusted to see that someone had shot a young tom-cat, the kind that we used to call New England barn cats, a big grey striped cat,' Russell says.

'I knew that a lot of hunters and conservation officers routinely shot cats that were straying into hunting areas. I understood why one might decide a cat had no business trespassing, but I could not forgive the carelessness of a hunter who would not be certain of his target and leave an animal to die a lingering death.'

Russell pointed his shotgun at the dying cat. 'I would at least put it out of its misery. He had been shot in the throat, and whenever he tried to make a sound, bubbles of blood formed and burst around the hole in his neck.'

His finger tightened around the trigger. 'But then I looked into its eyes and it seemed as though I received some kind of telepathic request for mercy. I put the shotgun on safety, leaned it against a nearby tree-trunk, and bent down to take a closer look at the wounded tom.

'Upon a more complete examination, I made a layman's assessment that the cat might have used up a couple of its nine lives, but with a little humane care it would probably live. The bullet, small calibre, perhaps a .22, had passed completely through his throat without causing a great deal of damage – other than setting free a lot of blood.'

Not truly understanding why, Russell picked up the tom-cat, carried it back to his pick-up, and brought home a bloody, furry surprise to his wife Donna.

Within a week, the Russells had the young tom up on his feet and eating hearty meals. The only permanent injury was to the cat's voice. One night he began to miaow for the first time since Craig had brought him home, and both of the Russells started laughing at the bizarre sound the cat produced.

'He honks like a Canadian goose!' Donna said, giving her impression of the strange, coughing noise that the cat emitted.

'He sounds like a very bad trumpet player,' Craig laughed. 'I hope when Gabriel the archangel appears on Judgement Day, his trumpet sounds better than that.'

The Russells burst into renewed laughter at the pleasure of realizing that they had just discovered their pet's name: Gabriel.

Gabriel did not complain or seem resentful that his peculiar honking 'miaow' almost always precipitated some form of amusement for the Russells or their guests. The tom-cat just seemed happy to have found a home, and he spent every evening curled up beside Craig's chair, as if keeping a watchful eye over the human who had saved his life.

'He seemed to love watching me work,' Craig says. 'I had begun writing some freelance articles on outdoor life and hunting. I had been having some luck selling a few pieces, and I would sit every night after I had finished working at my "real" job at the supermarket and bang away at the typewriter. Gabriel would sit and watch me strike those keys by the hour.'

Gabriel maintained that protective gaze for over thirteen years. Then one night in July 1980, the tom-cat just kept looking at Craig when his master made repeated calls for bedtime.

'Gabriel died a very peaceful and gentle death,' Craig Russell says. 'Those loving eyes just kept staring at me without blinking after I called him and called him to come to bed. Finally I knelt down beside him and found that he had died while watching me finish another article for a wildlife magazine.'

Two years later, Craig received his first big, all-expenses-paid assignment from a popular sports magazine. He was to travel to a newly opened resort area in a northeastern state and write a review of the place's facilities. He was warned that the conditions would be a bit rustic and rough, but life in northern Minnesota had equipped him for the wild.

The resort sought to capture the flavour of an early 1900s hunting lodge, and Craig felt that the effect they had achieved was quite accurate and ruggedly charming. He would spend the next day hiking in the woods around the resort proper.

'I fell into a dead sleep,' Russell says. 'I had put in a very full, and rather strenuous, day. But I was awakened in the middle of the night by Gabriel's unmistakable honking trumpet blasts. At first my dream mechanism fitted the sounds into a wonderful dream scenario in which Gabriel was not dead but was with me.

'Then I sat bolt upright in bed, remembering where I was. Once again, I clearly heard Gabriel's "horn" honking away at me to get up.'

Russell pulled on his trousers, slipped on his boots, and opened the door to discover the hall outside his room filled with smoke. He had barely escaped from the hallway when a sudden draught from somewhere in the lodge literally ignited the area with an explosive blast.

'My room had become a tinderbox. I couldn't even step back into it to get my suitcase or my clothes. Fortunately, I had on my trousers and boots, and someone handed me a coat. Everyone thought it was a miracle that I had awakened in time to escape the fire. The men on either side of me had not been so fortunate.'

While a rural fire department worked to save the remainder of the lodge, Russell stood quietly looking up at the moon, allowing the tears to course freely down his cheeks. He knew that his old friend Gabriel was still watching over him with his protective feline gaze.

BLUE ANGEL BATTLED EVIL GHOST CAT TO SAVE OWNERS' BABY BOY

A few years ago, a yong couple of my acquaintance rented an old house in a medium-sized city in Wisconsin before moving to their new split-level home. For several consecutive nights after they had moved into the old house, their two-year-old daughter would awaken with screams of terror.

The solicitous mother would carefully examine her daughter in an attempt to determine exactly what could cause the child such anxiety. After a week, the girl refused to sleep in her own room, and her parents were forced to move her into their bedroom for the four months that they remained in the house.

'There *was* something about that one particular room,' the father told me. 'After I took the time to investigate a bit, I could definitely understand why Jennifer refused to sleep in there. At night, when I was getting ready for bed, I found myself glancing toward that door, as if I expected someone – or *something* – to come walking out.'

The mother confided in me that she had once felt something brush across her ankles when she was in the room. She described the sensation seeming like an invisible cat brushing up against her ankles. Although such a sensation might be described as being somewhat pleasant under ordinary circumstances, she said that the feeling had filled her 'with absolute loathing, as if some repulsive creature had reached out and touched me'.

It was not until the young family had moved into their new home that they learned that an elderly recluse and his three ageing Siamese cats had once lived in the old house. According to the account that they were told, the recluse had first poisoned his cats, then hanged himself in the bedroom that they had used for their daughter's nursery. Several previous tenants had also complained of something odd being centred in that particular room.

As eerie as their experience may have been, my young friends' encounter with a ghostly cat pales in comparison with an account of an evil phantom feline that was given to me by Henry and Carol Salvato of Houston, Texas.

It was in May 1975 that the Salvatos acquired the key to the house that seemed to have been built just for them. Both Henry and Carol felt that it was a stroke of good fortune that had delivered the magnificent old home in the Houston suburb into their hands. They never doubted they and their children, seven-year-old Sandi and eleven-month-old Steven, would be happy and secure in their new home. And there was also a spacious garden for Blue Angel, their four-year-old Russian Blue cat, to romp in and climb trees.

But pleasant as the house had initially appeared, and as neatly as the Salvatos had furnished it within, after the first three or four days, both Henry and Carol became sensitive to an air of foreboding that seemed to hang over the place. And neither of them could ignore Blue Angel's strange behaviour in certain rooms. Once, the cat had arched his back and growled at some irritation that was invisible to them.

Hoping to dispel the gloomy atmosphere, they telephoned Father Martin Thalheimer to call on them and deliver a traditional blessing to the house.

The priest, a man in his mid-fifties, seemed cheery enough until he paused in the hallway outside a spare upstairs bedroom. 'Something gave me a bit of chill there.' He smiled apologetically. 'I'm glad . . . very pleased that you asked me to give the blessing to your new home.'

On the first weekend they spent in the house, the Salvatos were awakened by a slamming door. Henry and Carol sat upright, she reaching out instinctively to protect the baby that slept between them. They listened in the darkness, and from somewhere in the house they once again heard the sound of a door slamming.

Henry told his wife that a door must be caught in the wind.

To himself, he wondered if the wind could turn the knob on a latch door, then open and close it.

He slipped out of bed to investigate the noises. Although a man of uncommon courage with a distinguished record in Vietnam to prove it, Henry admitted that the eerie sounds had not only bewildered him, but made him feel uneasy.

As he stood in the kitchen, he heard a series of scratching sounds, which seemed to him to be very much like the noise of a scrambling animal as it scurried for cover.

Blue Angel stood fast beside him, glancing quizzically about the room, his vivid green eyes seeking to penetrate the mystery of the strange sounds.

'I don't see anything, either, Buddy,' Henry said to his cat. 'Where are those noises coming from? And what the hell is making them?'

Blue Angel answered with a low throaty growl that startled Henry. The cat was normally quiet, almost shy. It was so out of the ordinary to hear him growl.

At the sound of Blue Angel's warning yowl, the noises in the kitchen suddenly stopped.

The silence itself seemed almost to be a prelude to something even more bizarre and unsettling, but Henry smiled and said: 'Hey, boy, you scared off whatever it was!'

A defiant thud sounded from the ceiling above them, as if in contemptuous response, then all was silent once again.

From that evening on, the Salvatos were visited nightly by an array of sounds. The greatest concentration occurred about midnight, and no matter how the doors had been secured, they banged to and fro as if they had a will of their own. Eerie whispers of half-words and snatches of nearly understandable phrases echoed in the air around them whenever they went to investigate.

Both Henry and Carol were growing to believe that such nocturnal manifestations could have no natural explanations, and they began to understand why the magnificent house had been standing empty for so long and why it had been so cheap. Their dream home was beginning to transform itself into a nightmare.

'We could see that Blue Angel's sensitivity made him very susceptible to the phenomena,' Carol says. 'He would arch his back and hiss and spit whenever he walked into the bedroom above the kitchen, which was where the manifestations seemed most concentrated. We were thankful that Sandi appeared unaffected by the haunting – or at least we thought she was.'

One afternoon while Carol was straightening her daughter's room, she found a number of long white cat hairs on her bed. She knew that the hairs could not be Blue Angel's, for his plush blue coat yielded only short, dense, fine hair.

When she enquired of Sandi whether or not she might know anything about the strange hairs, the child's answer made her shiver.

'I guess they must be from the big white kitty that comes and sits on my bed every night, Mommy. Blue Angel is terribly jealous of her, and he always chases her away whenever she comes to play with me.'

When the Salvatos heard about the white ghost cat that was materializing on their daughter's bed, they made the decision that Sandi would begin sleeping in their room.

'Thank God we had not put her in the bedroom where the greatest concentration of supernatural power occurred,' Carol says. 'We almost did make that Sandi's room because it was so bright and sunny during the day. But one evening when we had come back to inspect the house just before we moved in, it had felt so gloomy and oppressive.'

Loud, inexplicable bumps and thumps issued from the haunted bedroom every night, but after the third week of the Salvatos' occupancy, they also began to manifest occasionally during the day – and in other areas of the home.

Once when Carol was cleaning the kitchen, she felt a cold draught and what she described as 'icy fingertips' running over her body. Almost immediately coincident with the onset of the peculiar chill, she felt what she at first believed to be Blue Angel rubbing himself against her ankle.

'I distinctly felt something soft and furry rubbing against my leg, and when I saw that it was not Blue Angel and remembered that he was upstairs with Sandi, my whole body began to shake with fear and revulsion.'

Carol told herself resolutely that if she refused to fear such manifestations, they could do her no harm.

Henry reasoned in nearly the same manner. Even though there appeared to be a sense of evil that had clearly presented itself to the Salvatos, both were certain that fear of it would only give it greater power over them. Both of them had been reared Roman Catholic, and they considered themselves to be religious and spiritual people.

'Carol and I told ourselves that only those who feared supernatural forces could be harmed by them,' Henry says. 'We firmly believed that to be a reasonable assumption.'

One hot night in early June, the Salvatos were awakened by Steven crying out between them on the bed. Blue Angel appeared to have been disturbing the baby, and Henry snatched up the cat quite roughly. He was in the process of removing Blue Angel from the room when Sandi cried out that their friend had just saved Baby Stevie.

'The big white cat was sitting on Stevie's face!' Sandi said, beginning to cry. 'It was trying to hurt the baby. The white cat is not nice. It let me play with it, but it is not nice. It wanted to hurt our baby! Blue Angel jumped up on your bed and chased the bad cat away.'

Carol nearly became hysterical at the thought that their son could have died from supernatural suffocation.

And both Carol and Henry were horrified at the notion that whatever evil presence infected the house had actually been bold enough to manifest between them and attempt to claim the life of their child.

'We've got to call Father Thalheimer in the morning,' Henry declared. 'We must ask him to perform an exorcism and rid this house of whatever evil lives here.'

The next evening, after the rite of exorcism was completed, Father Thalheimer crossed himself then addressed the Salvatos.

'The ceremony to purge the house has been performed,' he said, softly. But then a worried look came to his features, and he added, 'The performance of the rite, however, is no guarantee that the spirits will not return.'

At that instant a tapping came on the ceiling, and Carol looked up in fear before falling into the arms of her husband, whose face was set in an expression of grim determination.

When the tapping had ceased, Father Thalheimer continued speaking. 'I would have called you had you not summoned me. I have recently completed some enquiries about the history of this house, and I must inform you that there is evil here.'

According to the priest, the previous owners had moved out of the house after the tragic death of their baby due to suffocation under mysterious circumstances.

'The child had been in perfect health,' Father Thalheimer continued his account. 'The child's death had occurred on a warm night in June, and the family had used no bed covers. There were no marks on any kind on the infant, yet it had died of apparent suffocation.'

Henry felt his wife's hands gripping his arms. Carol was trembling in fear.

'Like yourselves,' the priest said, 'the previous occupants of this house, and certain of their visitors, had reported seeing the manifestation of a large white cat.'

Carol could no longer repress her tears nor the expression of her concern. 'If it had not been for Blue Angel, our baby might have been suffocated last night as he slept between us.'

'There is more,' the priest said, his voice becoming unsteady as he spoke of evil and violence. 'The original owners of this house were said to have been practitioners of the dark arts. After they appeared to have died in some kind of ritual suicide, it came out that during the course of their evil practices they had abused several children from the area. The death of their own infant son may actually have been a sacrifice to Satan, rather than an accident, as it had been officially decreed. Both of the Satanists had dyed their hair white and had a number of white cats that they appear to have sacrificed on a regular basis.'

Carol Salvato's features appeared pale and wan. 'Why

weren't we given any of the history of this place before we moved in?'

'That's obvious!' Henry replied with a derisive burst of laughter. 'Who in their right mind would buy such a place?'

'Leave this unholy house!' Father Thalheimer said. 'Take your children and leave at once.'

Henry shook his head. 'It's just not that easy. We put every cent we had into this house. We can't afford another until this one's sold. And that,' he laughed wryly, 'probably won't happen again in our lifetime! No one wants to buy a house that kills kids!'

Henry looked to his wife, then to the priest. 'No,' he said resolutely, 'we will not be driven from our house by nasty spirits. We cannot allow whatever infects this house to defeat us. We can't!'

As if in retort, the inexplicable tapping began once again on the kitchen ceiling.

Glancing upwards, Henry continued speaking: 'We will stay strong in our faith. If we keep fear from us and stay in the light of God, we can beat whatever is in this house.'

'Then my prayers will be with you,' Father Thalheimer said. 'I will ask that God grant you peace from whatever spirits dwell in this house.'

Two nights later, however, the evil within the house focused itself into an irresistible force.

Henry Salvato had been upstairs shaving while Carol worked at some household task on the first floor. Although he had been experiencing some distinct feelings of unease, Henry did not become conscious of the foreboding whispers which floated through the air until they had surrounded him with greater volume than he had previously heard. They seemed to encircle and close in on him until the suggestion of evil became so strong that he feared for his wife.

Dropping his razor, Henry rushed to the stairs where a frightening scene awaited him. Carol stood on the landing, transfixed with terror. Her limbs had stiffened and her hands clutched frantically at her side. The veins along her neck had swollen and were darkly visible. She had her head thrown back. Her eyes bulged with fear, and her mouth gaped in a scream that could not be heard.

Henry knew that he must help her, but when he moved down the stairs he ran into an invisible force that would not allow him to pass. It seemed to shroud him like an unseen net, holding him fast, while his hands desperately flailed the air and his feet worked futilely.

At last one of his hands found the banister, and with that as a lever Henry summoned all of his strength to hurl his body into the palpable wall of evil.

He broke through with a lunge, and instantly, the sounds of his wife's screams filled the house.

The next moment, he stood by her side, holding her close as she sobbed into his shoulder. She, too, had been gripped by the whispering evil and seized by its terror.

Sandi!

As if in that same speechless instant both parents were alerted to the danger that faced their daughter, Henry and Carol ran back up the stairs and into their daughter's room.

Sandi was cowering in a corner, tears streaming from eyes that were widened in terror. Standing just before her, his back arched, his green eyes glowering defiance, his warning growl indicating his resolve, Blue Angel provided determined interference for whatever evil stalked his young mistress.

The Salvatos had had enough. Without bothering to pack, they grabbed Sandi and Steven and left the house – with Blue Angel running just behind them, as if covering their retreat.

A week later when the Salvatos returned with some friends in the bright light of an afternoon to collect their belongings, they, took, heard the strange whispers and thumping sounds. Once they had finished packing, the Salvatos said that they would sustain a severe financial loss rather than ever enter that house of evil again.

In more than thirty years as a chronicler and researcher of the strange, the unusual and the unknown, I have found that certain houses can act as reservoirs of emotions from past occupants, and that certain rooms can become psychically charged storage batteries. Nearly everyone has had the experience of walking into a 'happy' house, a 'depressing' room, or a room that appeared quite ordinary in every respect until it seemed suddenly to trigger distinct impressions of unease or distaste.

Sensitive animals, such as the dog and – especially – the cat, can perceive these impressions and may be unable to interpret them as anything other than a threat to themselves and their owners.

Sensitive humans, those possessed of the proper telepathic affinity with the implanted memory-patterns of a particular environment, may enter a certain room and receive an influence from those who have lived there before. They may experience the emotions, share the impulses; and if the impressions are strong enough, even catch 'glimpses' of the former inhabitants, i.e., ghosts.

As yet our science is inadequate to define precisely what factors must be present before a dramatic haunting – such as the one the Salvato family experienced – can occur. For the present, we must theorize that a psychic impregnation is somehow made on an environment by a living, physical entity in a state of emotional intensity. Therefore, a certain house or room could be so 'charged' that even years later those same impulses could be received and experienced by a sensitive human – and responded to by a sensitive animal.

Some researchers hypothesize that extreme emotional states, such as great sorrow, overwhelming fear and intense hatred, increase the 'radiation' of these influences and make their primary and secondary results more powerful. An extreme emotional experience, such as that of a murder which took place in a paroxysm of hatred and terror, would be expected to create the deepest psychic impression and have the strongest power to evoke similar emotions in a percipient. It may then be put forward that some houses, due to the highly charged emotional level of certain deeds of violence or enmity perpetrated within their walls, have become repositories of hatred and reservoirs of evil.

Fear, sorrow and hatred, unfortunately, seem to be

stronger emotions than happiness and contentment. While a sensitive person may feel warm and secure in a 'happy' room, it seems seldom that one ever gains any clear impression of what made that particular room so joyful.

Or is it the dark side of our personality that is most easily reached by psychic impressions? Fear, Edgar Allan Poe believed, was the most primitive of emotions and the easiest to evoke in a fellow human. It is a sobering thought to contemplate that what we may leave behind us after we are gone is our worst impression.

THE HORNED CAT CREATURE THAT SAT AT THE TOP OF THE STAIRS

John Pendragon, the late British clairvoyant and seer, told me the following eerie account of a demonic ghost cat while we were collaborating on his biography, *Pendragon – A Clairvoyant's Power of Prophecy* (Tandem Books, London, 1968).

It was a very distressed Howard Leland who came to Pendragon one October afternoon in 1943. Perhaps more than anything else the man wished to receive validation of his supernatural experience and to be told that he was not going mad.

'I have been a volunteer with the ARP, the Air Raid Precautions, and a couple of nights ago during a raid, I took shelter in a deserted house in south London,' Leland began his account of his frightening encounter. 'I sat on the bottom step of the staircase, and after a few minutes I had the uncomfortable feeling that something was watching me from the top of the stairs.

'I clicked on my torch and flashed the beam upwards. I was startled half out of my wits to see a blackish-brown, hairy creature that looked like an extremely large tabby cat squatting on the top stair – and the bloody thing had horns sticking out of its head!'

Leland paused to measure a distance from his forehead to

indicate the approximate length of the protuberances. 'And the monstrous thing had long, sharp-looking claws, too.

'The wretched beast and I stared at each other for fully half a minute,' Leland continued. 'I shall never forget the evil that shone in those eyes! I'm not ashamed to admit that I was too scared either to advance or retreat.

'Then the hellish cat thing, whatever it was, leaped from its squatting posture and seemed to jump into an empty room. I could hear it yowling and howling about.'

At that point, Leland said, two pals of his entered through the open front door. He explained as best he could what he had seen; and, strangely enough, they did not laugh at him or start on him about drinking on his watch.

'One of my mates told me that the hideous creature had been seen off and on in the neighbourhood for years,' Leland said. 'Previous residents of the house had witnessed the thing. Always, it seems, the monstrous cat creature was seen sitting at the top of the stairs – in the very same spot that I had seen him.'

At that point Pendragon interrupted him. 'Did you or your friends go upstairs to look for any physical signs to corroborate your story?'

Leland nodded. He had felt more courageous in the company of his companions, and they had gone upstairs to investigate.

'We found not a thing,' he admitted, shaking his head.

Then he narrowed his eyes and wagged a forefinger for emphasis, his voice rising to a near shout. 'But I *did* see that creature on the stairs and no one can convince me otherwise! I am not subject to hallucinations – and I most certainly had not taken a drink that night.'

Pendragon laughed softly. 'There's no need to convince me. I shall be happy to take your word for your encounter.'

'Then can you tell me what I saw, Mr Pendragon?'

'What interests me,' the clairvoyant said, 'is *why* the creature was there. Please give me the address of the building.'

Pendragon wrote down the address on a slip of paper

and concentrated on it for several moments. No impression came.

He rose from his desk and stood before a large-scale map of London that he had tacked to the wall. Looking closely at the map, he located the building in question – just a tiny dot amidst the thousands of dwellings in south London.

The moment Pendragon placed his forefinger on the minuscule dot, he suddenly 'saw' the darkened stairway that was the lair of the hideous horned cat creature.

Something moved from the shadows. Not a creature, but a man. A despondent man who had sought to better his position in life by engaging in the practice of black magic, an endeavour that had included the ritual sacrifice of dozens of cats on his perverse satanic altar.

Pendragon's highly developed psychic abilities permitted him to view a most extraordinary recreation of a past event. Swirling about the devil worshipper as he walked towards the top of the stairs were the spirit forms of the many cats whose hearts had been ripped from their bodies by the cruel sacramental dagger. Pendragon reeled in a moment of vertigo as he felt the hatred of dozens of feline psyches focused on their murderer.

Then the clairvoyant noticed that the man carried with him a rope in which he had fashioned a noose. There was a brilliant flurry of macabre images, and Pendragon suddenly felt a violent constriction of his throat. Coughing spasmodically, he removed his forefinger from the map and reached for the cup of tea on his desk.

'If you will make enquiries,' Pendragon told Leland after he had allowed the soothing tea to calm him, 'I am certain that you will find that a previous resident of the house committed suicide by hanging himself from the banister at the top of the stairs.'

'And the cat creature?' Leland wanted to know.

'Yes,' Pendragon nodded, 'it is there. It is quite likely an elemental spirit that has assumed the general form of the dozens of cats that this disturbed gentleman sacrificed on his satanic altar.'

'An elemental?' Leland echoed. 'And what's this about satanic rites and all?'

'A man hanged himself in utmost despondency when his attempt to better himself through the black arts failed,' Pendragon explained. 'This poor wretch had even resorted to animal sacrifice, slaying dozens of cats on his makeshift satanic altar. Elementals are prone to frequent places where a tragedy – generally suicide or murder – has occurred. They are also associated with places where black magic rites have been performed. They are most certainly a sort of personification of evil.'

Pendragon recalled that Howard Leland returned to his office before the end of a week.

'I don't know how you managed to peg it,' Leland told him, 'but I learned from long-time residents in the neighbourhood that a previous resident did indeed hang himself from a banister.

'Before the man killed himself,' Leland continued, 'folks said that they had been bothered by the sounds of cats yowling and screaming from the house in the middle of the night. And it was shortly after the man's suicide that people started seeing that terrible horned cat thing at the top of the stairs.'

Leland concluded, 'I guess there really are more things between heaven and earth than are dreamt of in anyone's philosophy!'

SPIRITS OF CATS THAT CAME BACK TO GIVE COMFORT

My late colleague Professor Ian Currie was not only a respected professor at the University of Toronto in Ontario, Canada, but he was also a world-renowned psychical researcher who had investigated sightings of spirit entities for many years.

'Ghosts of cats are very much like ghosts of humans,' he

said. 'I believe that they return from the afterlife primarily to give comfort to grieving loved ones that they've left behind.'

There was the case of the woman in Toronto who lost the Persian cat that she had adored for seventeen years. Her entire family was in mourning for the beloved pet, for they all knew how much their mother had loved and cared for him.

On the third evening after the cat's passing, the woman was awakened in her bed by the sound of her Persian's familiar purr of affection. With tears of joy streaming down her cheeks, she next felt the delicate touch of her cat's tiny feet moving over her shoulder as he prepared to snuggle around her just as he had done in life.

The next morning at breakfast, she came to the table filled with excitement over her experiences of the evening before and eager to share the good news of her cat's return. But before she could utter a word, her daughter was telling everyone of her own marvellous encounter with the world beyond death. The cat had visited her during the night, as well.

Within a few more days, the spirit of the Persian cat had manifested as a ghostly apparition that had been seen by many witnesses.

'I have seen him come through the wall from my daughter's room,' the ghostly cat's owner revealed. 'His eyes shine like jewels, and there is a bluish light and little star-like sparks all around him. He bumps me in the face and gives me his soft little kisses.'

Professor Ian Currie cited the impressive case of an English aristocrat, Sir Ernest Bennett, who had become extremely attached to his pure-bred Persian named Smokey.

Depressed and saddened by Smokey's death, Sir Ernest and his sister were startled to observe the very distinctive Persian cat limping across the lawn outside their mansion. Smokey appeared to be ill, but she was unmistakably the beloved cat that they had lost to physical death.

Sir Ernest ran outside to reclaim his dear Smokey – but the cat vanished.

Could they have both been seeing things? Sir Ernest questioned over and over whether both he and his sister had somehow projected their sorrow into the fashioning of some hallucination.

But then a family friend insisted that he had seen Sir Ernest's Persian cat walking the grounds of the estate.

In desperation, Sir Ernest instructed his gardener to disinter Smokey's grave to be certain that she had truly died.

Later, after the apparition ceased to manifest, the Bennett family conjectured that the times when they perceived Smokey's ghost were times when she was still confused and unaware of her death.

Psychic News, an international newspaper on spiritual matters published in London, has reported for years that the ghosts of dead cats often return from another dimension of reality to visit the human families that they have left behind on the earth plane. According to their many published accounts, ghostly cats have jumped on their owners' bed at night, materialized on their laps, and left nose smudges on windows.

One cat owner wrote to *Psychic News* to testify that his deceased cat's frequent visits from beyond the grave filled him with a great feeling of peace and love.

Another woman testified that a ten-minute materialization of her cat from the Other Side had enabled her to shake off an illness that had been lingering on far too long. Within two days, she was feeling better. Not only had her physical condition improved, but her fortunes had also taken a more positive turn.

THE CAT THAT SPOKE IN TONGUES

Although we raised the question of the possibility of demonic possession of cats in the chapter dealing with 'mean and scary cats' and chose to skirt the cosmological implications of non-physical entities assuming control of a physical body, there was a most interesting case in 1978 in a small town in New Mexico in which the family came to believe that their large Siamese cat was possessed by the poltergeistic activity in their home.

The word *Poltergeist* in German means a ghost that throws things; and in the parlance of contemporary psychical research the term has come to represent a paranormal disturbance characterized by explosive psychokinetic manifestions, i.e., objects being tossed about, mysterious fires breaking out, large pieces of furniture being moved and so on.

The manifestations that beset the Brian Clancy home began on what had been a quiet evening in mid-January. The initial demonstration of the unseen energy force had startled members of the Clancy family who watched a ceramic flower pot lift itself from a shelf and crash through a nearby window pane.

During the evening meal, a sugar bowl floated up to the chandelier and dumped its contents in the electric candle holders. Pictures tumbled off their hooks and crashed to the floor. An old brass incense burner flew six feet off a bookshelf. Some recent acquisitions of Native American pottery that had been left on a bed were smashed to pieces by an unseen force. A case of soda bottles exploded like a string of firecrackers. A small table in the dining room suddenly became animated and danced on two legs across the room. ‑

And then the pebbles began flying.

Small multicoloured stones appeared out of thin air and began to pelt Brian and his wife Mary and their two children, Angela, twelve, and Sean, five. Angela and her Siamese cat Bonnie Jean seemed to be struck the most often, but very few of the pebbles landed with enough force to raise a welt or bruise. It was as if the stones floated towards them.

By the time the police arrived, a barrage of rocks was falling on the roof of the Clancy home. The officers listened to the various family testimonies with bemused expressions of disbelief. Although they could hear stones dropping on the roof –

but could see nothing 'because it was dark out' – they concluded that some birds must be dropping pebbles as they flew over from desert areas. They promised to have an animal control officer come by in the morning to check things out in the daylight.

After a night of iced-tea glasses shattering, ashtrays smashing themselves against walls, and a stack of firewood exploding and sending bits of bark and pulp across the room like wooden shrapnel, Brian Clancy placed a much firmer call to the authorities.

The police department's crime laboratory could find no trace of any explosives having been inserted in the moving or exploding objects.

City highway personnel tested for earth tremors with a seismograph and found nothing.

A friend of Clancy's, a radio and television repairman, blamed the trouble on high-frequency radio wavelengths, but his sensitive equipment could record none.

And then, that night, Bonnie Jean, Angela's four-year-old Siamese, suddenly began to scream like a banshee. As the family stood by watching incredulously, the cat began writhing across the floor as if she were a snake – and making a loud hissing sound to complete the impression.

But the most horrible, and seemingly impossible, manifestation occurred when a bizarre kind of babble began issuing from the Siamese – gibberish that sounded for all the world as if it was a jumble of human tongues.

'We could not prove that Bonnie Jean was saying words,' Mary Clancy says. 'But it did seem as though the cat was speaking in tongues. I have never heard such sounds coming from the mouth of a cat!'

Angela continued to hold her pet in her lap, attempting to soothe it during its most dramatic gyrations. 'Bonnie Jean's eyes rolled around in her head, and she made these terrible noises,' Angela says. 'She acted a lot like the little girl in the movie *The Exorcist*.'

Bonnie Jean acted so much like the possessed girl in the movie that Brian Clancy contacted their pastor, who offered prayers, but who quickly bowed out when he heard the cat hissing and saw it writhing like a snake.

'He said that the matter was beyond his theological expertise,' Mary recalls. 'And he didn't even hear Bonnie Jean speaking in tongues.'

Bonnie Jean's harsh guttural roars and screams were becoming louder, and with the increased frequency of the 'speaking in tongues' aspect of the phenomena came a barrage of airborne objects, such as knives, forks and stones directed at Angela. Although the twelve-year-old was not seriously injured by the missiles, she was thoroughly frightened by her role as the target for an invisible throwing ghost.

For those who read such accounts as the eerie experiences of the Clancy family, it may all seem like a combination of trickery and hallucination, intensified by the power of suggestion. However, witnesses to such poltergeist activity are very often highly educated and responsible persons who have perceived for themselves unexplained sights and sounds – objects that move without any traceable causes and, in some cases, rappings and voices that exhibit intelligence.

The late psychoanalyst, Dr Nandor Fodor, believed that there was no doubt that the poltergeist was a part of our world of reality. Basing his beliefs on his investigations, he pointed out that the life-time of a poltergeist was usually limited to a few weeks or months. The poltergeist becomes, as it were, an unbidden guest, moving in to work its pranks and horrors upon an unappreciative family.

The difference between a *geist* (ghost) and a *poltergeist*, in Dr Fodor's evaluation, is that a ghost haunts a house and the poltergeist haunts a person. 'The poltergeist is not a ghost,' he stated, 'but a bundle of projected repressions.'

Not all researchers agree with Dr Fodor that a poltergeist always has to do with the repressions of the living and never with the anger or frustrations of the dead; but the majority of psychical investigators probably do agree that the centre of the poltergeistic activity is usually associated with a teenage member of the family, more often a girl than a boy. An exhaustive study of poltergeist manifestations convinced noted researcher Harry Price that the sexual changes inherent in puberty are frequently associated with either the beginning or the cessation of the phenomena.

Sacheverell Sitwell has written his opinion that the poltergeist finds its centre of energy in the person of an adolescent, who performs the effects, both consciously and unconsciously, 'being gifted for the time being with something approaching criminal cunning. The particular direction of this power is always towards the secret of concealed weaknesses of the spirit . . . the obscene or erotic recesses of the soul. 'The mysteries of puberty, that trance or dozing of the psyche before it awakes to adult life, is a favourite playground for the poltergeist.'

Whether or not the poltergeist that visited the Clancy family shifted its 'playground' from Angela to Bonnie Jean, the Siamese, must remain the subject for academic and esoteric conjecture.

A Navajo medicine priest and healer, summoned by the Clancy family, declared that the evil spirit of a snake-worshipping cultist from long ago had possessed the cat. The medicine priest performed a lengthy ritual of chanting and prayer that, he explained beforehand, was designed to bring the entity peace and to free it to travel on to the land of the grandfathers.

'Whatever the man did, it seemed to have a calming effect on Bonnie Jean and upon the disturbances in our home,' Brian Clancy says. 'The cat's growls, grunts and roars grew quieter. And that bizarre babbling sound it emitted ceased altogether.'

Bonnie Jean appeared to fall into a deep sleep as she was cradled in Angela's arms, and when she awakened after ten minutes or so, she looked up at her young mistress and began to purr.

'Hey, everybody,' Angela smiled. 'Bonnie Jean is back. She's her old self again.'

Whatever the power of the Navajo medicine priest's ritual of exorcism – or whether the energy of the poltergeist had simply expended itself – the Clancy family's ordeal had ended.

CURSE OF THE CAT MUMMY IN ENGLAND'S OLD MILL HOTEL

Local residents of Sudbury, England, believe that some kind of ancient curse was set upon them when a mummified cat was removed from beneath the floorboards of the historic Mill Hotel during renovations and not quickly and properly replaced.

When builder Arthur Kemp found the mummified feline, he was puzzled about its possible significance. He could tell that it was very old, and he wondered if some taxidermist of ages past had hidden away a particularly significant stuffed cat for some long-forgotten purpose.

Local historians to whom Kemp brought the mummified cat told him that it was a common practice centuries ago to imprison a live cat in a new building to protect it from evil spirits.

'It was a sort of sacrifice,' one old-timer informed Kemp. 'About 300 years ago, it was a regular thing to lock up a cat so that its spirit could keep the evil ones away. I've found about a dozen or so in other old houses and hotels in this area and I always put them back where I found them. I would advise you, sir, to do the same thing!'

The owners of the Mill Hotel found the bit of local folklore that Kemp brought them to be most interesting, but they decided to put the mummified cat on display in an art shop they owned.

'Don't you think we ought to pay some attention to the old-timer's advice?' Kemp asked them. 'Why don't I just put the old puss back where I found it?'

The hotel owners had hired Mr Kemp because he had been highly recommended as a fine builder. They politely informed him that they did not require his services as a decorator. The mummified cat would stay on display in the art shop, thank you!

A few weeks later, the art store burned down. The cat mummy stood silent and erect among the smoking ruins – not a hair of his ancient coat so much as singed.

Kemp learned later that the mummy was given to a friend of the owners who lived in a farmhouse outside town. Within a few weeks, that house was also severely damaged by a mysterious fire that broke out round the mummified feline remains.

Incredibly, the hotel owners then gave the mummy back to Arthur Kemp – who, even more incredibly, accepted it. The builder was not keen on placing the object in his home or in his office, however. He decided that he would keep it in the boot of his car to see if he couldn't temper the power of the curse.

He temporarily forgot about the old mummy due to the pressure of his work – and then had three car accidents in a week.

At the same time that the mummified cat was bringing him grief from the supposed security offered by the boot of his car, he heard that the section of the Mill Hotel where he had discovered the centuries-old remains had collapsed. Once again, Kemp was called in to handle the repair work.

Just before Kemp was able to get at the task, the old hotel was taken over by new owners, who were much more receptive to the builder's account of the curse of the cat mummy. They didn't want any part of the bad luck that had been circulating ever since the remains were disturbed. They even asked Kemp to construct a special niche for the mummy and to place it back under the hotel floorboards where he had found it.

Once the builder had respectfully – if not reverently – replaced the mummy beneath the repaired floorboards, things in Sudbury seemed to return to normal.

According to the old Mill Hotel's present manager, the power of the curse appeared to have been appeased and there was no more trouble after the mummy was returned to its former resting place.

But then, he had to admit, as unwise as it should have seemed, he decided to give the mummy a good, hygienic cleaning.

That night the sprinkler system in the kitchen mysteriously

came on, drenched the place, and caused thousands of pounds' worth of damage.

'I'll never touch the creature's mummy again,' the manager vowed. 'It is apparent that every time the mummy is disturbed, misfortune is certain to follow.'

CHAPTER SEVEN

CATS WITH WEIRD TALENTS

On a November night in 1989, the police in Tulsa, Oklahoma, were puzzled by an emergency call that seemed to be nothing more than moans and a high-pitched yowling; but the computer display system showed them the exact address from which the call was coming.

When Officer Dale Ferber arrived on the scene, he found a darkened house in which no one responded to his ringing of the front doorbell or his follow-up vigorous knocking.

Fearing the worst, Ferber called for backup; and the two officers received authorization to break in through the front door.

Once inside the house, the officers heard the reported moaning and yowling – only they were clearly able to identify the sounds as those of a troubled cat! When they entered the kitchen they found a very anxious Simba the Siamese all tangled up in a twelve-foot telephone cord and lying on the floor next to a toppled counter telephone.

'In its struggles to get free,' Officer Ferber says, 'the cord had tightened about the cat's throat. If it hadn't dialled 911, it would have strangled itself in a very short time.'

And how had Simba managed to dial the police emergency number?

'The way we figure it,' Officer Ferber explains, 'the Siamese must have jumped up on the counter, got tangled in the telephone cord, fell to the floor, and pulled the phone with him. When cat and phone hit the floor, the receiver got knocked off; and as the cat struggled more and more to free

himself, he stepped on the button that had been preprogrammed to dial 911.'

Simba's owners, Allan and Jayne Horn, had been to dinner
and a movie, and they were startled to return home to find
their front door badly damaged and a note of explanation
from the police.

The Horns expressed their gratitude to the officers for
having saved their cat's life. 'A new door we can always get,'
Jayne Horn says, 'but our Simba is one in a million.'

On 20 October 1990, police in Troy, New York, broke into an
apartment after their 911 emergency number had received
what sounded like a call from someone too injured and weak
to speak. But when they got inside, they found to their
astonishment that the caller must have been saying, '*Miaow*' –
not 'Me . . . *ow!*'

Bill Krauss's cat, Yeager, had apparently pawed the pad of
a preprogrammed push-button telephone that automatically
dialled the police emergency number. Although the dis-
patcher heard no intelligible voice, he was able to trace the
call to Krauss's apartment.

When the officers who were dispatched to the scene of the
supposed emergency couldn't find a building superintendent
or break down the door, they cut through a window screen.
Once inside they found no terribly injured accident or crime
victim, just a contented cat named Yeager, who had obviously
been playing with the telephone.

Bill Krauss thought that it was someone's idea of a weird
joke when he returned to his apartment to find a note tacked
to his door. According to Krauss, the note basically said the
following: 'Your cat called the police. We had to force entry to
check the apartment.'

Police Sergeant Robert Paul said that no charges were being
contemplated against Yeager the cat for filing a false report.

Marvalee Wagner of Alameda, California, said that her cat
Rusty is an accomplished thief of people's underwear and
socks.

'Rusty really has a thing for laundry,' Ms Wagner says. 'She steals sweaters, hats, undies – but she's especially fond of socks!'

Once, Ms Wagner said, Rusty went on an all-out weekend raid and brought home forty-two socks, mostly ladies' knee-highs.

Ms Wagner said that she had long since given up attempting to track down the victims of her little desperado. She just piles the stolen socks and assorted laundry at her front door, and the neighbours come over and reclaim their stolen articles.

Missy, a Siamese with a flair for tap-dancing on computer keys, was performing an intricate fandango on her owner's home computer in Los Angeles when she accidentally punched in a secret five-letter code that accessed a business memory bank – and instantly erased $50,000-worth of account files.

A company spokesman, decidedly not an aficionado of Siamese dancing, stated that they would have to revamp their entire computer system.

Gypsy attained local fame in Washington, DC, for being a feline alarm clock. The black and white tom-cat awakens his mistress at precisely 6.45 a.m. each morning – and is even able to make the necessary adjustments for Daylight Saving Time.

Sally Longbaugh joins the ranks of those many cat lovers who claim to have a feline that speaks actual, discernible words in brief phrases.

'Beau clearly says, "Let me out", "I love you", "Eat now, Mommy", and several other phrases,' Ms Longbaugh says.

Raymond Long insists that he has built up a strong telepathic link with his cat Fred that enables them to communicate even at a great distance.

'Once when I was in Baltimore on business,' Long says, 'I received the distinct impression that there had been a small fire in our apartment. I felt Fred's fear and his consternation. I could feel that he wanted me with him. I also saw that he had my most expensive wristwatch – one I never take with me on the road – in his bed with him.'

That night when Raymond telephoned the friend he had asked to check on Fred, she told him that there had, indeed, been a small fire in his apartment building.

'I think it was two or three floors below your place,' she said. 'I could tell that old Fred was pretty shook up about it, though. You know, the smoke and the sirens and everything. And a funny thing, Fred had your favourite wristwatch in his mouth when I came to feed him. It was like he was going to save your most valuable belonging in case of fire.'

Henry Craig is among those cat lovers who vow that their felines have the remarkable ability of 'astral travelling', that is, leaving their physical bodies to be seen elsewhere at the same time.

'On several occasions, my fiancée has sworn that she has seen Burt in her place when he is curled up at my feet sleeping,' Craig says. 'My mother, too, has insisted that she has seen Burt watching her from the shadows when she goes to bed some nights. I know that he astral projects in his sleep and that his soul body looks in on those people that we both love the most.'

THE ASTRAL AWARENESS OF CATS

In their book *Psychic Phenomena*, Dorothy Bomar Bradley MD and Robert A. Bradley MD tell of a bachelor friend of theirs, a great cat fancier, who had a black cat as his companion for many years. Throughout the course of their relationship, it had been the cat's habit to run to the refrigerator whenever it was hungry and pace back and forth in front of the door while miaowing its desire for food. When their friend had occasion to move to one particular apartment, however, the cat would not go near the refrigerator – even if the most tempting food was being proffered there.

The Bradleys' friend informed them that his cat seemed to be afraid of that area and would sit and stare at the refrigerator for long periods of time. When the bachelor described his cat's peculiar behaviour to his landlady, the woman offered the explanation that the former tenant had been a widow who had disposed of the refrigerator and the stove and elected to eat all her meals out of the apartment. In the recessed area where the refrigerator had stood, she placed a small table with candles. In the years before her own death, she had conducted seances at that spot in which she communicated regularly with the spirit of her deceased husband.

The Bradleys theorize that their friend's cat may have possessed an 'astral awareness', that is, an 'instinctual function . . . of the subconscious animal brain' that enables it to pierce the barrier 'between the unobstructed and obstructed universe, between the astral world and the earth world'. The cat in the apartment, lacking human reason and a logical, conscious mind, did not know how to accept the entities that it perceived and became frightened by the strangeness of the situation. Although it was used to the physical friends of its master, the cat could not deal with the sight of non-corporeal entities that made no sound and carried no identifying smells.

Lyall Watson, author of the acclaimed bestseller *Supernature*, related in his book *The Romeo Error: A Meditation of Life and Death* the following account of an experiment involving the varying abilities of animals to perceive the unknown.

Summoned to investigate an allegedly haunted house in Kentucky, Robert Morris of Duke University brought with him a collection of living 'ghost detectors' in the form of a dog, a cat, a rat and a rattlesnake. One by one, each of the animals was taken by its owner into a room in which a murder had once been committed.

The dog walked only two feet into the room, then uncharacteristically began to snarl at its owner and backed out of the door. No amount of cajoling or promised rewards could induce the dog to re-enter the room.

The cat's owner carried her pet into the room, and when it reached the same spot where the dog had turned tail, it leaped up on to its owner's shoulders. A few moments later, it jumped to the floor, directed its attention towards a corner of the room, and spent several minutes hissing and spitting and staring at an unoccupied chair.

The rat showed no signs of sensing anything, but the rattlesnake instantly coiled into an attack stance while focusing on the same empty chair.

'None of the three responsive animals produced a comparable reaction in any other room of the house,' Watson writes. 'The relative acuteness of the cat's sense system may account for the fact that witches use them as familiars, as aerials or extensions of their own senses for picking up subtle signals.'

A MYSTERIOUS CAT APPEARED TO FREE HER FROM THE GRIP OF A TERRIBLE NIGHTMARE

Catherine Layton experienced an eerie, foreboding sensation the moment she set foot in the lovely seaside cabin. Although the day was bright and sunny, both the kitchen area and, more especially, the bedroom, seemed dark and sinister even though dazzling sunshine streamed through the open windows.

'Is this the only cabin that's available?' Catherine asked Mrs Pickron, the landlady, who seemed to be avoiding eye contact with her.

'You know this is our busiest season,' the tall, thin woman answered by way of indirect reply to the pointed question. 'Just about everybody wants to be on the beach in July. I told you when you wrote that you were lucky that we had any vacancies. We've got a waiting list, you know, so if you don't want it . . .'

The implied threat was very thinly veiled. It was just that Catherine was disappointed in the sombre and somewhat oppressive atmosphere of the seaside cabin. She had so looked forward to a pleasant two weeks in a new and different location where she might receive some positive inspiration to write a number of freelance magazine articles. Fifty weeks out of the year, as society editor for a small-town newspaper in Illinois, she wrote about weddings, engagements, graduations, Rotary dinners and funerals – for two weeks she wanted to write for herself. That was why she had decided to holiday in this quaint resort town on the Virginia coast.

'No, no, the cabin is fine,' Catherine assured Mrs Pickron. 'It's just that it feels . . . strange to me.'

The landlady arched a defensive eyebrow and compressed her lips into tight, bloodless lines before she answered. 'My husband Lester and I work hard to make these cabins pleasant and cheerful. I gave you Cabin Sixteen because it is one of our loveliest. Maybe it's the ocean that troubles you . . . the sounds of the waves and all. Takes some Midwestern folk – who normally hear only cricket and critter sounds – a while to get used to the noise of the surf.'

Catherine knew that there was no need to explain to the dour and touchy landlady that she had lived in Illinois for only four years. She had grown up in La Jolla, California, with the sounds, smells and rhythm of the surf an integral part of her body, mind and spirit.

'I'm certain that I will adjust,' Catherine said. 'The cabin is fine.'

Mrs Pickron permitted herself to smile, perhaps more in triumph than in satisfaction, and even offered to help Catherine carry the rest of her luggage into the cabin.

'In order to keep the budget tight, I had already decided to cook most of my meals at the cabin,' Catherine states in her account of her remarkable experience. 'But on my first night by the ocean, I made up my mind to treat myself to an elaborate meal at an elegant seafood restaurant I had passed a few miles back. I returned to the cabin about three hours later, full of excellent lobster and exquisite wine.'

Although the evening temperature was quite warm, upon her return to the cabin Catherine noticed at once that its interior felt cold and damp.

'But I had driven over three hundred miles that day, and my understandable fatigue, coupled with the good food and the wine, made me think about nothing else but collapsing into bed and getting a good night's sleep. Tomorrow morning would bring a beach walk, some sun and a good session at the typewriter.'

But the night did not bless Catherine with a restful sleep.

'In a terrifying dream scenario, I was lying in bed when I heard a strange shuffling sound. I looked up to see a dark, human shape coming towards me from the kitchen. It was one of those really nasty dreams – you know, the kind where you can't move and you can't run and you can't even scream. This thing kept coming closer and closer, and then I could hear that it was calling my name over and over.

'It smelled of seawead and brine, and as it bent over me I could see this horrible skull-like face leering at me.'

Catherine awakened drenched with sweat, strands of her hair matted to her damp forehead. 'I blamed the bad dream on too many glasses of wine,' she admits, 'but I got up, went to the bathroom, then turned on every light in the cabin before I could go back to sleep.'

The dream haunted Catherine all during the next day. She took her beach walk, lay in the sun for twenty minutes or so, then tried to work on one of the articles for which she had been taking notes for the past fifty weeks.

'I decided not to be too hard on myself. After all, the days before my holiday had been exhausting. The editor had insisted that I cover every Fourth of July function in town and have all the copy on his desk before I left on the sixth. And then there had been the straight-through drive from Illinois to Virginia, stopping only for catnaps at the safest-looking rest areas. I really owed it to myself to spend at least one day doing nothing before I got to work on the article.'

That night, in spite of a pleasant evening spent in delightful conversation with the young honeymooning couple in the cabin to the left of hers, the awful nightmare returned to terrify her.

'This time I seemed to have a telepathic link-up with the rotted corpse from the sea,' Catherine says. 'It . . . he . . . had once lived in the cabin. He had stayed there frequently with his wife. Then there had been a terrible fight, a nasty, shouting argument, over her acts of infidelity. At last, she admitted her unfaithfulness and scornfully laughed at him, mocking his ineffectualness as a lover. Humiliated, he had run out on to the beach and into the pounding surf. An undercurrent caught him just a few yards out, and he had drowned.

'It was becoming clear what he wanted with me,' Catherine continues her story. 'Fiery red eyes glowed lustfully in the empty skull sockets. Since all women were nothing but sluts in his warped view, he now sought to prove himself an effective and virile lover with every woman who occupied that cabin. The same cabin that had served as his stage for heartbreak and humiliation would now for ever be the plat-form for the proving of his eternal manhood.'

Catherine found herself trying desperately to awaken from the grip of the terrible nightmare. 'I could not seem to wake up! And he had begun to press his cold, wet claw-like fingers into my shoulders. Seawater and saliva dripped from his partially decomposed lips as he brought his ghastly face closer and closer to mine. I could feel him beginning to move his sea-drenched body on top of my own. And all about me was the salty stench of the sea.

'At last, with a supreme effort of will, I managed to awaken, to free myself from the cold grip of the ugly, obscene, animated corpse.'

This time, at four o'clock in the morning, Catherine could not blame the hideous nightmare on too much lobster and too many glasses of expensive wine.

'What concerned me most was the horrible thought that if I should have the dream again, would I be able to wake up?' she says. 'I suddenly felt as though I was in a movie like *A Nightmare on Elm Street* and a monster as bad as Freddy Krueger was trying to get me while I dreamed. Would I have to try to stay awake and not dream, like the teenagers in that movie?

'And if I should fall asleep and dream and be unable to awake in time, would I somehow be imprisoned within the nightmare until the wretched, horrible thing had had its way with me? And even worse, might I somehow be trapped inside the dream for ever and never awaken?'

Catherine brewed herself some strong coffee, drank several cups, then went outside to spend the few remaining hours until dawn on the beach.

By the first light of dawn, she was chiding herself for allowing an overly active imagination to transform her into a frightened wimp. What nonsense! Being trapped inside a dream while a lustful corpse tried to have its way with her.

If she told Mrs Pickron about the nightmares, she would blame it on a Midwesterner having a hard time adjusting to the sound of the pounding surf. If she confessed the dream to the honeymooners, barely out of their teens, they would snigger and whisper behind her back that she, an old maid of thirty-five, was no doubt sexually frustrated.

Still, as much as she allowed the process of rationalization to chatter on and on inside her brain, there was something so strange, so real, so terrifying about those nightmares.

It was precisely at this moment of pure reason and abject fear that Catherine felt something soft and furry rubbing against her bare ankle. Startled out of her interior monologue, she could not suppress a small squeal of relief when she beheld the exceptionally large Maine Coon cat that had joined her.

'In the two days that I had been there, I had seen a number of dogs running on the beach, but not one cat,' Catherine says. 'I had no idea where this one had come from, but his company was most welcome.'

The sort of person who is compelled to give a name to every creature large and small that makes her acquaintance, Catherine called the large cat 'Buddy'.

'Buddy followed me back into the cabin and did not hesitate to accept the food that I offered him. Within a few minutes it was obvious that he was making himself at home. Somehow I felt better already, just knowing that I would not face the night alone. My Buddy was there with me.'

The cat stayed by Catherine's side throughout the entire day, joining her on a beach walk, gingerly approaching the foaming surf as it broke on the sand.

'When we met Mrs Pickron and her husband Lester on the beach, neither of them could ever remember seeing Buddy – or any cat that looked like him – in the area before,' Catherine says. 'Lester offered that he, himself, "fancied" dogs.'

That night when she pulled back the blankets to get some sleep, Buddy jumped up on to the chair next to the bed and assumed a position of vigilance.

'It was the strangest thing,' Catherine says. 'Buddy showed no signs of intending to sleep. It was as if he were on guard duty.'

Weary from lack of rest because of the night before and calmed by the presence of her guardian, Catherine permitted herself to drift into a deep state of relaxation. Within moments she had fallen fast asleep.

'I must have slept for hours. I had a number of brief dreams about my work back on the newspaper, and I was in the midst of a pleasant memory recreation of a summer trip to Yellowstone Park that I had taken with my parents when I was around thirteen when I suddenly became aware of a dark, shadowy form following me,' she says. 'A cold hand reached out to grab my arm, and I was pulled back to the Virginia seashore. I was thrown on my back on the coarse sand, and then *he* was on top of me, pinning my arms above my threshing head, pressing my struggling body to his evil will.

'Waves of nausea surged over me as his rotting lips tried to find my own. I knew that I must wake up. I must free myself from his nightmarish hold on me. I must summon all of my will power to escape from him.'

Catherine remembered how the entity laughed at her puny efforts to resist his amorous advances. '"It's no use," he laughed at me. "I have you now!"'

That was when she became aware of Buddy yowling into her ear, and she felt herself momentarily jerked from the terrible grip of the demon in her nightmare. The obscene entity roared a string of blistering profanities, then pulled her back into the awful dream.

'I was suddenly the object of an incredible tug-of-war,' Catherine says. 'I wanted to wake up and be free of the nemesis from the nightmare, but the terrible creature's hold on me had become too great to enable Buddy's screeches to awaken me fully. My guardian must have sensed this, because that was when he bit me hard and deep on my shoulder. The pain seared through my nerves and slammed hard into my brain, shattering the ghastly dream into a million pieces of harmless unreality.'

Catherine sat up in her bed and opened her eyes to perceive the most beautiful sunrise she had ever seen in her life. She had escaped from the terror of the night. Her guardian cat had somehow sensed her incredible dilemma and acted to free her from the demon's grip with the most immediate means at its disposal.

'It didn't quite seem to be over,' Catherine says. 'The large cat appeared to be chasing something into a shadowy corner of the bedroom. He sat up on his haunches, pawed the air with his claws extended, and emitted one of the loudest, most startling cries that I have ever heard come from a cat's mouth.

'Buddy must have sent the evil thing packing with that fierce battle cry, for he got back down on all fours, and seeming quite satisfied with himself, walked to the kitchen to lap at the bowl of milk I had set out for him earlier in the evening.'

A short while later, as Catherine was fixing some breakfast for herself, Buddy jumped up on to the kitchen counter and brought his head close to her own. 'He seemed to be focusing his large green eyes on mine, and almost as though I were hearing words directly in my brain, he was telling me that everything was all right now. I was safe. The nightmare would not return.'

Catherine cradled Buddy in her arms and began to weep. 'His pink little tongue touched my cheek twice, then he jumped free of my arms and headed towards the cabin door. I called after him, but he kept walking, mindful of his own schedule of activities, his own mission in life.'

She never saw Buddy again. 'I spent some part of every remaining day looking for him,' Catherine says. 'I asked about him, but no one ever recalled seeing a large Maine Coon cat anywhere on the beach.

'I'm convinced that Buddy appeared solely for the purpose of freeing me from the nightmare's demonic control over me. Maybe he was my guardian angel.'

For the remainder of her holiday, Catherine slept soundly, her dreams untroubled. She also managed to complete three articles to her professional satisfaction.

It was during checkout at the main desk on her final day at the cabin that Lester Pickron provided her with the capper to the whole affair.

'Well,' he smiled expansively, 'I guess you beat the jinx of Cabin Sixteen.'

Catherine frowned as she echoed his words about a jinx, and she noticed that Mrs Pickron was nowhere to be seen.

'Yeah, the missus and I called it a jinx, anyway,' Lester acknowledged before he explained. 'About five or six years ago, we had a nice young woman die in her sleep in that cabin. The doctors could never find any reason for her death. She just up and died. Ever since then, though, every single gal who rents that cabin has complained of awful nightmares and refused to stay more than a night. It's been a really weird thing, because we never told any of the other ladies about the woman's strange death. We've tried to keep it quiet, that's for sure.'

Catherine entertained a brief thought of throwing Mrs Pickron into the ocean.

'Anyway, Miss Layton,' Lester smiled again, 'thanks for breaking the jinx.'

Catherine wanted to tell him to thank a mysterious Maine Coon cat that had somehow heard her silent prayers for help and had come to her rescue – but she knew that neither of her insensitive hosts would ever be able to understand.

THE HEALING POWERS OF CATS

Hundreds of cases document the astonishing healing powers of cats. They have been reported bringing children out of deep comas, helping the mentally ill achieve renewed stability, and bringing new hope to those who had accepted only pain and despair as their lifelong companions.

Judy Kaplanis had always believed that her fourteen-year-old tom-cat Rodney had a special gift for making her feel better. Mrs Kaplanis had had Rodney since she was sixteen, and he had always had the knack of cheering her up whenever she was gloomy or depressed.

'There was just something about that big old yellow cat that always made me feel good,' she says. 'And then, a few years ago, I begin to notice that not only would Rodney chase my blues away, he would take away my headaches and upset stomachs.

'My kids noticed it, too, because they started calling for Rodney to sleep with them whenever they were coming down with a cold or had a stomach ache. Even my husband Jim picks Rodney up and sets him on his lap when he comes home extra tired from work. After about an hour of stroking Rodney's yellow fur, Jim always says that he feels better and more invigorated.'

Judy has said that visitors to their home, who might not feel so well when they arrive, usually leave feeling greatly improved.

'A friend of mine suffered from terrible insomnia,' she says. 'Night after night she would toss and turn something awful. Well, one day she came to visit, and Rodney jumped up on to her lap. She didn't seem to mind, so I just let him sit there so I could see what would happen. When I saw her three days later, she said that she had been sleeping at nights like a baby.'

A local school administrator suffered so badly from arthritis that she feared that she would be forced to resign her position before the end of the term. After one visit to the Kaplanis home and after holding Rodney on her lap for a while, the administrator's condition was so much improved that she is able to lead a normal life.

On occasion, Rodney's presence has healed other cats, dogs, even parakeets.

'Some people may think that I'm crazy talking like this about Rodney,' Judy says. 'But I truly believe that my cat has the gift of healing.'

Gretchen Tynar from Scottsdale, Arizona, relies on her Persian cat Prince to relieve her minor aches and pains.

'If I have a bad sore throat, Prince knows intuitively to drape himself across my neck when I lie down,' she says. 'My throat will feel better in minutes. The same is true if I have a stomach upset, a backache, or a headache. The moment I lie down, Prince goes immediately to the part of my anatomy that is troubling me.'

Gretchen believes that Prince absorbs the pain, then releases it in another dimension of reality. 'I know that this will sound really weird, but I have watched him walk into a particular corner in the sitting room of my apartment – and just disappear. I mean, like that, he is gone.

'Then maybe in an hour or less, he'll be out in the hallway scratching at the door to be let in. There is no way that he can get out of the apartment except through the door, and I keep it locked at all times.

'So how do you explain it?' she asks. 'How can he walk

into a corner of the sitting room, disappear, and a few minutes later be out in the hall? My healing cat is also a multidimensional cat!'

OWNING A CAT CAN LOWER YOUR BLOOD PRESSURE

Owning a cat can slash your risk of heart disease, lower your blood pressure, and reduce cholesterol levels, according to a study of more than 5,000 patients conducted by Dr Warwick Anderson of the highly respected Baker Medical Research Institute. Dr Anderson stated that pet owners had significantly reduced risk levels for cardiovascular disease.

A University of Pennsylvania study of heart attack victims showed that owning a pet can mean the difference between death or recovery. Doctors found that simply stroking a cat can reduce blood pressure and heart rate. The rhythmic process of petting a cat can achieve the same effect on a stressed out patient as certain relaxation techniques such as meditation.

Dr Leo Bustad of the College of Veterinary Medicine at Washington State University has expressed dismay that it has taken such a long time for people to become convinced of the value of animals such as cats in improving human health. Pets have amazing healing powers, Dr Bustad commented, and their very presence seems to be able to block pain.

Researchers have theorized that the bond that develops between a cat owner and his pet is focused on the process of touching – and in many instances that may be the real key to a cat's healing powers. Very often the mentally ill have isolated themselves from the touch of other human beings. Sometimes a patient with a debilitating disease has been deprived of a loving touch for far too long. The cat with its friendly purr is much less threatening than another person, who may respond to a loving gesture with a rebuff and rejection.

A recent survey conducted by Dr Erika Friedmann of Brooklyn College revealed that the survival rate for heart patients with a pet is much higher than for those without animal companionship. Dr Friedmann is also disappointed that such awareness comes so slowly for too many patients, who want a magic drug in a capsule, rather than a loyal and playful cat.

JANE BAILEY'S REMARKABLE FELINE HEALERS, ROGAN AND GUS

British spiritualist Jane Bailey has been privileged to serve as the human catalyst for two remarkable feline healers, Rogan and Gus.

In the early 1970s, Ms Bailey began to notice how people with illnesses appeared to feel so much better after her cat Rogan had spent some time with them. It seemed to her that Rogan had been blessed by some higher power with the gift of healing.

Rogan even attended church services with his mistress. It reached the point where the vicar could count on Ms Bailey and her pet always taking the same spot in the fourth pew on the right. And it amazed the clergyman to see the cat bow his head at appropriate times during the service, especially when a prayer was announced.

It appeared that Rogan loved attending church services. Whenever Ms Bailey would take him for a walk, he would begin to strain at his leash, hoping to go in every church that they passed. There was no question that the devout cat seemed happiest when he was healing people and when he was sitting in a church.

'With just a laying-on of his paws, he actually cured a woman friend of mine who was suffering from chronic depression,' Ms Bailey recalls. 'On another occasion, Rogan miraculously cured a clergyman's severe asthma.'

Rogan did not always have to be present to serve as the channel for healing energy. Once, when the owner of a desperately ill Persian cat came to them for a healing, Ms Bailey and Rogan went to church, bowed their heads together in prayer, and sent healing energy to the afflicted feline.

In a few days, Mrs Bailey received a letter from the Persian cat's mistress stating that her pet was vastly improved and that the puzzled vet who had recommended that the cat be put to sleep was 'utterly awestruck'.

In seeking an anecdote that would illustrate the power of the love energy that flowed through Rogan, Ms Bailey remembered the time that a distraught, nearly hysterical woman approached her at a charity event, declaring that she could not take any more of life and that she wished to die. Ms Bailey suggested that the woman sit in the car with Rogan for a few minutes. The cat crawled on to the weeping woman's lap, then stood up on his hind legs, put his forepaws on her shoulders, and gazed into her eyes.

The once-distraught woman said that a great peace came over her. The headache that seemed as though it might blind her suddenly disappeared – and the feeling of inevitable doom that had terrified her for months vanished for ever.

Rogan lived to a ripe old age but, as every physical entity must, he eventually moved on to a higher dimension of service. But Ms Bailey continues to help people with their troubles and traumas through the agency of a four-year-old tom-cat named Gus.

'I am convinced that Gus was sent to me by the spirit world to carry on in Rogan's pawsteps,' she says.

As many as seventy seekers of healing per day come to the home of Ms Bailey and Gus.

'These people pay nothing for their healings,' she says. 'Some of them feel better after merely stroking Gus. Sometimes he jumps on to the patients' laps and gives them eye-to-eye contact. After a few minutes they leave feeling totally free of pain and anxiety.'

In one press account, Canadian rheumatologist Dr Raj Patel was quoted as stating that he had referred five patients with degenerative knee-joint disease to Gus. 'And in each of these patients, the degree of severity was such that I truly believed that they were not amenable to correction. You can imagine my astonishment when these people – seemingly crippled for life – visited Gus and then almost danced into my office.'

In Dr Patel's assessment, to describe Gus the cat as a healer would be to 'grossly understate his credentials'.

In Ms Bailey's cosmology, Gus is in contact with spirits, and he channels their other-worldly energy to help those people and animals who are sick and who need his loving services.

WOULD YOU BELIEVE — FLYING FELINES?

Back in 1959 there were all kinds of excitement about a flying cat in Pinesville, Virginia, and the ruckus over the bizarre beastie spread throughout the entire United States.

It seemed that Thomas, who was really a female but who was named before the biological fact was discovered, had developed a true biological rarity: he had wings. And for ten cents, you could line up and see this wonder of nature for yourself.

Fifteen-year-old Douglas Shelton, who captured the winged feline while hunting in the hills, had nearly shot the critter before he identified it as a cat.

After he had shinned up a tree and caught it, Douglas discovered that the animal had two bizarre lumps growing out of its back. Upon closer examination, Doug saw that they were wings. And when he touched them, the cat got mad and started clawing at him.

Other than a decided touchiness about his wings, Thomas had pretty good manners, and he seemed right at home with the Shelton family. Word spread fast about Doug's winged cat, and it wasn't long before a reporter from the Beckley,

West Virginia, *Post-Herald* was there to examine the oddity with an objective, journalistic eye.

For her many eager readers, Fern Miniacs described Thomas – whom she quickly identified as female – as looking very much like a somewhat large Persian cat with long, beautiful hair. The wings were furry and soft, she noted, but had a feeling of grittiness near the body.

'It's thirty inches long,' Ms Miniacs wrote, 'has a tail like a squirrel, and two perfectly shaped wings, one on each side. The wings are boneless but evidently have gristle in them. Each wing is nine inches long.'

A veterinarian who journeyed all the way from Baltimore to identify the growths on Thomas' back confessed, after a rigorous examination, that he had no idea how to explain the unusual biological occurrence of a cat with wings.

Thomas even had his day on NBC television's *Today* show. On 8 June 1959, Doug told Jack Lescoulie, who was filling in for the regular host Dave Garroway, that he had been offered as much as four hundred dollars for the incredible cat, but he was not tempted in the least to sell her.

At the height of Thomas's national notoriety, a quiet, unassuming widow named Mrs Charles Hicks, who lived on the Pinesville–Baileysville road, stepped forward and announced that the cat belonged to her.

The soft-spoken, grey-haired lady insisted that she did not wish to make trouble for Douglas Shelton or anyone else. She just wanted her cat back.

When reporters came to get her side of the story, Mrs Hicks told them that the cat that Douglas called Thomas, she had christened Mitzi. A friend had bought the cat in California and given it to her as a present. All of her neighbours, she insisted, had become used to the sight of Mitzi and her wings, and every one of them could substantiate her story.

'One day I put some medicine drops in Mitzi's ears,' she told the journalists. 'Mitzi didn't like that and she ran away. That Shelton boy found her four days later.'

When Douglas Shelton refused to acknowledge Mrs Hicks' claim, she sued him for the return of Thomas/Mitzi.

On 5 October 1959, Doug appeared in circuit court with a large Persian cat under one arm and a cardboard box under the other. The first thing that everyone in the courtroom noticed was that the cat Doug Shelton carried most certainly had no wings of any description.

In embarrassed tones, young Shelton told the judge that Thomas had 'shed' her wings in July. With a dramatic flourish, he opened the cardboard box and revealed two large clumps of fur.

'There they are, your Honour,' he said. 'There are Thomas's wings.'

Mrs Hicks indignantly proclaimed that the large Persian cat that Douglas Shelton had brought into the courtroom was *not* her Mitzi.

Ignoring the widow's protests and accusations of feline substitution, the judge awarded her one dollar in damages 'for her trouble', and gave Doug Shelton full custody of what now appeared to be a most ordinary Persian cat.

The maelstrom of publicity over Thomas the Winged Cat evaporated as quickly as it had begun. Doug Shelton and the big Persian cat disappeared into obscurity, and whether or not – as Mrs Hicks suggested – the *real* winged cat flapped her bizarre appendages solely for the edification of Doug and his friends, the two of them seem never to have been heard of again.

In his fascinating book *Strange Creatures from Time and Space*, John A. Keel recounts the tale of Thomas and Doug and goes on to detail an account of a large black feline with ostensibly functional wings that was said to terrorize the community of Alfred, Ontario, in June 1966.

On Friday, 24 June, Jean J. Revers, a confectioner, was startled by a creature that he described as 'looking like a big black cat – but with hairy wings on its back'.

Revers told authorities that he had observed the astonishing flying feline swooping down after a neighbour's more conventional landlocked cat.

The winged cat had 'screamed like hell' as it tried to get

away, Revers said. It took 'gliding jumps of fifty or sixty feet – wings extended – after a good running start.' He insisted that the creature could remain a foot or so above the ground.

Revers fired five bullets into the howling, fluttering feline freak as it attempted to attack his neighbour's cat.

Police Constable Terence Argall told investigators that he could not believe his eyes when he examined the thing that Revers had killed: 'Its head resembled a cat's, but a pair of needle-sharp fangs five-eighths of an inch long protruded from the mouth. It had a cat's whiskers, tail and ears, and its eyes were dark, greenish and glassy. I never saw anything like it before in my life.'

Further examination revealed that the flying feline had a wing-span of fourteen inches. Its pelt was sleek black, and it weighed about ten pounds.

According to dispatches from United Press International, another flying cat was shot near Lachute, a village located north of Montreal.

During June 1966, at least three large black flying cats were reported in villages in Ontario and Montreal. Did someone forget to close the back door of the Twilight Zone?

KIKI — THE DEVA-SHAN OF WAIKIKI BEACH

When is a cat not a cat? When it is a Deva-shan, a nature spirit, an elemental being disguised as a cat.

For fourteen very interesting years, Dr Patricia-Rochelle Diegel and her husband Jon-Terrance lived with their beloved Waikiki Beau, who was also known as the 'Deva-shan of Waikiki Beach'.

'You see, what has happened in Honolulu as the high-rises and the condos keep going up, is that the elemental spirits, the nature spirits, the Devas, are being pushed out of their natural habitat in the South Pacific Polynesian jungles,' Dr Diegel says. 'Consequently, in order to continue with their evolution, some of them must assume the bodies of certain animals, such as a horse, a cat or a Dalmatian dog.

'Why are those animals preferred? It seems to be because they all get kidney stones,' she says, 'though I don't know exactly what that has to do with it. Something about moving them higher up the evolutionary ladder.'

Jon-Terrance, a bishop in the Antioch Catholic church, added that he had been told that the elementals would now begin to seek the bodies of domesticated animals, which were more highly evolved than jungle creatures.

The Diegels first made the acquaintance of Kiki when two of their students brought him to a class in metaphysics that they were teaching in their bookstore in Honolulu.

'They had found this small black kitten with golden eyes wandering in the Ala Moana shopping centre,' Dr Diegel says. 'They felt the cat was very special, so they just could not leave him to wander the streets. Neither of them lived in apartment buildings that would allow pets, so they didn't know what to do with the stray cat that they had felt was so unique.'

But Kiki knew that he had found *his* humans. He jumped up on Patricia's lap, curled up on her shoulder, and slept peacefully there while she taught her evening class.

'At that time,' Jon recalls, 'Kiki was so small that he could fit in the palm of my hand. We stopped on the way home to pick up some milk and a can of tuna. Later that night, he slept on a pillow between us, a position he would maintain throughout his life with us.'

Immediately the Diegels noticed certain peculiar things about the cat that they had christened 'Waikiki Beau'. He did not miaow; he did not like to play 'kitty-type' games; and he did not bother the cages of birds that they kept on the balcony of their ninth-floor apartment.

In her research, Dr Diegel has observed that black animals are more highly evolved. 'And highly evolved cats don't miaow very much.'

One night Patricia-Rochelle was awakened by Kiki, who was obviously trying to tell her that something awful was afoot. She followed him to the balcony and there discovered that two stray cats had ascended to the ninth floor in hungry pursuit of Jon's caged birds.

'Kiki was not about to permit those stray cats to harm those birds,' she says. 'Those birds belonged to *him* and to Jon!'

Kiki also had the ability to speak certain words. Whenever he wished to be let out, he would approach one of the Diegels and say clearly, 'Me . . . out!'

'Numerous guests distinctly heard Kiki accent the "t",' Dr Diegel says. 'Kiki was not simply miaowing to be let outside. He was saying, "Me . . . out."'

The Diegels also began to notice that Kiki had powers of precognition in that he always knew which class member would not attend a session on a particular night.

'He would walk back and forth in front of the chairs assembled for class as if he were inspecting them, then he would jump up on the one particular chair of the student who, for whatever reason, would not attend that evening. And he was never wrong.'

Kiki also had the ability to detect potential students who were heavy drug users.

'If someone who was into drugs applied for class, Kiki would growl at them,' Patricia-Rochelle says. 'Since this came from a cat that almost never miaowed or growled, we took immediate notice. Kiki would look above them and begin to growl as if he saw that they were bringing along negative entities in their aura.'

When Sybil Leek, the internationally famous metaphysician and spokesperson for modern witchcraft, visited Honolulu, Dr Diegel could not resist telling her about their Kiki.

'We were seated on the balcony overlooking the pool at the Sheraton when Sybil went into a light trance,' Patricia says. 'When she opened her eyes, she declared that our Kiki was really a Deva-shan, an elemental, that had assumed the form of cat in its evolutionary ascent. She pronounced him to be the "Deva-shan of Waikiki Beach".'

It was about this time that the Diegels acquired Fang Lei to keep Kiki company.

'I had always wanted a dog so that I could name it "Fang",'

Jon says. 'A dog just wouldn't work out with our lifestyle, so I gave the name to a cat. When people stated that "Fang" was an Oriental-type name, I added "Lei" to round out the nomenclature.'

The Deigels noticed that Fang Lei was prone to getting lost or trapped inside places, such as the cupboard. Whenever his companion disappeared, Kiki would transmit telepathic images disclosing where they might locate Fang Lei and rescue her.

Some years later when the Diegels were renting an apartment in Los Angeles from one of Patricia-Rochelle's old school friends Kiki accomplished one of his most astounding astral projections and materializations.

'My friend Lois did not particularly care for cats,' Dr Diegel says, 'so I would leave Kiki in our apartment with Jon whenever I came to visit her. On this one particular occasion, I glanced up from our conversation in Lois's apartment to see Kiki walking in the hallway from the bedroom.

'As we both sat almost mesmerized, we watched Kiki walk into the room where we were talking, stand for a moment and look at me, then walk out the room and *through* the screen door.'

When Lois and Patricia went downstairs to the Diegels' apartment to investigate, they saw Kiki sleeping peacefully at Jon's feet.

'What are you two talking about?' Jon wanted to know. 'Kiki has been sleeping here for hours. He hasn't moved a muscle – and he certainly hasn't moved from this room.'

'Clearly,' Dr Diegel says, 'Kiki had visited us in his astral body. When he walked across the floor in front of us, he looked just as solid as could be. It was when he passed through the screen door that Lois and I knew that something was a bit strange about Kiki.'

Jon insisted that the cat had not budged from the room, so they could only conclude that Kiki had projected in his astral body to check in on Patricia upstairs.

The Diegels could write a book simply recounting all the paranormal experiences that they shared with their beloved

Kiki. The Deva-shan of Waikiki Beach left the physical plane when he was fourteen years of age. Fang Lei lived to be sixteen.

'We have decided not to acquire any new cats,' the Diegels told me as they prepared to move to Las Vegas in May 1992. Jon's most recent favourite, Shaun, had just died, the victim of a bobcat attack in Sedona, Arizona.

'We love cats so much,' Jon said, 'but they leave such big holes when they die. We probably will never own another cat.'

Although the Diegels have been our close friends for many years and they are truthful in all other respects, I knew that this was a vow that they would never be able to keep. At the time of writing, in November 1992, the Diegels own a 'positively Aquarian' mother cat, Shangri-La, and her beautiful litter of four – Shamballa, Madame Pele, Shasta and Indiana Jones.

We can only wonder how many of the above are really elementals, wood sprites or aliens in disguise!

ESTABLISHING A MIND-TO-MIND LINK-UP WITH YOUR CAT

It would be difficult to imagine more than three cat owners in the entire world who did *not* feel that they had experienced at least one telepathic link-up with their pets. Comments such as, 'My cat always seems to know what I'm thinking', 'I can call my cat just by thinking her name', 'I know that he understands everything that my husband and I say to him' are frequently heard whenever cat lovers get together.

We have already discussed the acute psychic awareness of cats in situations of hauntings and other paranormal activity, and we have noted that cats are the traditional 'familiars' of witches in the European tradition. Whether folklore or fact, cats are very often credited with exhibiting extensive extra-sensory abilities.

Just as the vast majority of cat owners believe that they communicate with their pets on some level of mental perception, there are a number of real-life 'Dr Doolittles' who claim that they are able to communicate directly with cats through their own ESP abilities.

Ann Rubenson of Ellsworth, Maine, states that she is a living 'psychic link' between people and their pets, and she considers it her responsibility to pass along various complaints that animals might have regarding their living conditions.

Ms Rubenson claims that she has heard cats and dogs complain about the names their owners have given them and even about being given hand-me-downs from previous pets. 'I have nothing of my own,' one cat griped.

Samantha Khury of Manhattan Beach, California, lectures on 'The Secret Life of Pets', urging her audiences to develop a stronger mental and emotional bonding with their pets.

'Close your eyes and picture your heart meeting your pet's heart,' she might say. 'Meet heart to heart, emotion to emotion. Let them convey their feelings, thoughts, and the very essence of their being.'

If your cat should have a bad habit that may be of particular annoyance to you, Ms Khury will instruct you to communicate with your pet through 'mental imagery'. Concentrate on the cat, think about its bad habit. Picture in your mind the manner in which you wish your cat to behave. Visualize your cat doing what you want it to do. Soon, Ms Khury offers, your cat will begin to pick up your mental wish and it will come to obey you.

If your kitten is ignoring the litter box and using your new Persian rug for her potty, Ms Khury suggests that you 'visualize her running for the box and defecating into the litter. Picture it urinating into the litter. Imagine the little sound it makes as it sprays. Get your cat's attention and tell her that you are thinking these things. She will understand that it is the right way to go potty.'

*

Mystic Meg, a British psychic sensitive who writes a regular column on metaphysical matters for the *Globe* newspaper in the United States, shares her life with seven cats.

'Once a cat has established a firm mind-link with you, it can track you down anywhere,' Meg affirms.

When Meg moved, she believed that her cat Ruby would much prefer to remain at home with Meg's mother. Although she would be separated from Ruby by 300 miles, the cat had spent her entire fourteen years in the family home, and Meg was certain that she would be more comfortable there.

However, the very day after Meg left home, according to her mother, Ruby stepped out of the door and disappeared.

Three months later, Ruby, no longer a chubby tabby, showed up exhausted but happy on Meg's doorstep at her new home.

In noting the telepathic ability of felines, Meg stated that as Ruby got older, she became deaf and blind. 'One of the younger cats, Alice, became her playmate and guide,' Meg says. 'Alice could always predict when Ruby needed her, and it is this same sixth sense that cats use to warn humans of disasters.'

Among Mystic Meg's advice on testing your own cat's psychic powers are the following tips:

While your cat is in another room, sit down quietly and slowly tense and relax your muscles. Breathe in and out slowly for a minute. Close your eyes and picture your cat coming to you in the room. If you have a true mind-link with your pet, she'll soon be there.

Hide a cat treat somewhere in a room. Bring your cat in and picture in your mind where the treat is hidden. Give her thirty seconds to find it.

In the September/October 1992 issue of *Body, Mind, Spirit* magazine, Barbara Rosen quotes animal communicator Penelope Smith as stating that your attitude towards animals more than anything else influences how willing they will be to communicate with you and how easily you will be able to 'hear' them.

'Many of us grew up believing that animals were "inferior" to us,' Ms Smith says. 'So we tend to talk down to them: "I am up here with a big human brain, and you are down there with a little brain. What can you send up to me?"'

Animal communicator Carol Gurney of Agoura, California, expressed her opinion that 'most animals like telepathy', but some may be shy, 'and others are very private and feel, "It's none of your business." And sometimes animals are just not in the mood to talk.'

Ms Gurney's advice to those cat lovers who really wish to tune in to their pet's thoughts is to learn to still their mind. 'If you have an endless stream of chatter going on inside your head, the animals will get a "busy signal" when they try to reach you.'

CHAPTER EIGHT

FIND YOUR IDEAL CAT IN THE STARS

'I believe that it is nearly as important to know your cat's sun sign as it is to know the zodiacal position of your future husband or wife,' one prominent astrologer told me not long ago. 'Look at it this way: the relationship that you will have with your cat will be very intimate, conducted in close quarters over a long period of time, and you must learn to trust and to respect each other.'

According to another successful astrologer with a celebrity clientele, the question of compatibility should be of primary concern before anyone decides upon a particular feline companion. 'By understanding the various character traits associated with the different zodiacal signs, you can better determine if you and the cat are going to get along!'

Practitioners of astrology maintain that our individual personality is determined by the pattern of the heavens at the time of our birth, plus our reactions, with relation to this pattern, to the stimuli found in our environment during growth and maturity.

Although I am by no means an astrologer, I have many close friends who are; and they have slowly convinced me over the years that there is *something* to be gained from the ancient lore of the stars.

I am most comfortable with those interpreters of the zodiac who claim that astrology is a science only inasmuch as mathematical plottings are used in the mapping out of horoscope charts. The rest of the astrological process constitutes an art, not a science – an art that provides its devotees with certain insights which may guide them around some rough spots in life.

In numerous conversations with professional astrologers, I have been assured that competent interpreters of horoscopes are capable not only of predicting certain trends in their clients' lives, but of also revealing a great deal about a person's character, personality and temperament. I have been told that often good astrologers need only the knowledge of the sun sign under which their clients were born to be able to produce such information. These same astrologers have also assured me that horoscopes can be cast for countries, corporations or cats, with the same kind of precognitive accuracy that can be achieved for individual clients.

If you know the birth date of the cat that you now own, the following exploration of the zodiacal signs is offered only in the interest of providing you with another possible tool to utilize in the building of a successful relationship between you and your feline companion. The information regarding the various sun signs has been compiled from numerous conversations with successful and competent astrologers, but it is being presented without claims of infallibility.

Your own inner sense about your potential relationship with the cat that you are considering acquiring should be the single most important determining factor as to whether or not you invite a new feline friend into your fold, not someone's interpretation of the stars. In the words of my dear friend, the late John Pendragon, a remarkable astrologer and clairvoyant from Tunbridge Wells, Kent, 'Astrology can be a very good servant, but an unreliable master.'

THE STARS AND YOUR CAT

The Aries cat – 21 March to 20 April

The Aries cat would prefer to rule the roost, so understand at once if you are considering obtaining a cat born under this sun sign that you may have to squash its desire to dominate.

The Aries cat generally has a strong resistance to diseases, and it is usually very robust. At the same time, it may be prone to accidents which affect its head.

If the Aries cat should succumb to illness, it will be inclined to run high temperatures, quite likely precipitating a visit to the vet.

The Aries cat prefers a rugged terrain. If you live in the mountains or in hilly country, your Aries pet will be in its element. If you are a city dweller, give your Aries cat a treat from time to time by taking it along on rides in the country. Just be certain that the air is brisk and keen if you should allow your Aries cat to wander on its own for a bit, for it will rapidly become tired and enervated in fetid, marshy terrain.

If you, the owner, should also happen to be an Aries, it will not be long before the feathers will fly between you and your Aries cat. If you already possess an Aries cat, you have no doubt already noticed a great deal of strife between you and your feline companion.

Those born under the sign of Taurus will have somewhat more patience with an Aries cat than would the Aries owner, but the Gemini cat lover would probably become quite annoyed with an Aries feline, as would the potential Aquarius, Virgo and Scorpio owners.

If you are born under the sign of Cancer, you would be very unwise to obtain an Aries cat. As a child of Cancer, you thrive on quiet affection and gentleness, and you will not receive such treatment from your Aries cat. If your sign is Libra, you would discover your temperament to be in decided conflict with an Aries cat. The same would hold true if you are a Capricorn.

A Leo owner and an Aries cat provide the best match. Although a Leo also likes to be in charge, he or she will not feel threatened by the aggressiveness of the Aries feline. If you are a Sagittarian, you stand the next best chance of getting along with an Aries cat. A Piscean's tolerant nature might also be able to adjust to the vagaries of the Aries feline.

The Taurus Cat – 21 April to 21 May

Although the Taurus cat would like to have its own way, it is not as demanding as those felines born under the sign of Aries. Taurean females make splendid mothers, and they will be extremely attentive to their litters.

Taurus cats have a tendency to put on a little too much weight, and they will be a little less judicious about overeating than other felines in the Zodiac.

Your Taurean will also love being cuddled and coddled. They are essentially love bugs, but they can become angered if provoked. Once they lose their tempers, they can become quite ferocious.

The Taurus cat is somewhat susceptible to throat troubles, and there is also a tendency for its glands to be upset every now and then.

Your Taurean feline will thrive best in an undulating countryside, well away from large bodies of water. An agricultural area suits the Taurus cat very well. Keep it away from areas of big industry. Your Taurean seems to draw energy from the woods and large clumps of plant life.

If you, the owner, happen to have been born under the sign of Aries, you will not have a particularly good relationship with a Taurus cat. You are likely to find a great deal of fault with the Taurean feline, and it will cringe under your dictatorship.

If you are yourself a Taurean, you will probably become impatient with your pet as it becomes older. You will be likely to be more affectionate with it in its kittenhood. Those potential owners under the signs of Gemini, Cancer, Scorpio, Sagittarius, Aquarius and Pisces are also liable to become annoyed with the mannerisms of the Taurus cat.

The Taurean cat will probably be happiest if its owner is an accommodating Virgo. A Capricornian or Leo could also accommodate a cat born under the sign of Taurus, but a Libran would be taking a bit of a gamble acquiring a Taurean feline.

The Gemini cat – 22 May to 21 June

You may have your hands full with a Gemini cat. It will quite likely be very intelligent, but it will also express a great deal of nervous energy – which can become very taxing. If you are an on-the-go sort, you will probably cherish your cat's seemingly inexhaustible energy.

That nervous energy, however, is likely to remain with your Gemini cat from kittenhood to maturity. You will also have to be aware that it is susceptible to lung problems. And like the Taurean cat, your Gemini pet may tend to overeat.

The Gemini cat functions best in an environment where it has plenty of room to run and to romp. You will also observe that, unlike other cats, your Gemini will seem to gain vigour from the wind and the rains. Life on the plains would suit the Gemini cat admirably.

A Gemini cat will get along very well with a Gemini owner, for they will keep pace with one another. An owner whose sun sign is in Aquarius would also be compatible with a Gemini cat. Another possible combination would be the Gemini cat with the Aries owner.

Libra, Cancer and Capricorn owners would probably enjoy the Gemini cat for a time, but there is a great danger here in the cat soon getting on their nerves. The same would probably be true of the Piscean and Taurean owners. A Scorpio owner would be well advised not even to attempt a union with a Gemini cat.

If your sign is Virgo or Sagittarius, there exists the possibility of harmony with a Gemini cat; but the happiest union probably lies in a Leo's acquisiton of the Gemini feline.

The Cancer cat – 22 June to 22 July

If you want a cat that will prove to be a great homebody, you can seldom do better than acquiring a feline born under the sign of Cancer. The Cancer cat may even seem somewhat lethargic, for it will exhibit little of the nervousness and restlessness displayed by certain other felines. You may notice, however, a slight fluctuation of mood during the full moon.

Basically a cat of cheery disposition, you may even see it shunning any family memeber or visitor who displays a gloomy or grouchy demeanour.

Your Cancer cat may come down with the occasional cold, and in its mature years will probably suffer from rheumatism. If you should wish to breed your female Cancer cat, have a vet check her generative organs and womb very carefully.

Although you won't find your Cancer cat enjoying a swim in a lake or the ocean, felines born under this sign do seem to have a certain affinity for water. A Cancer cat would love a home on the coast – or even near a marsh or a swamp.

The Cancer cat will respond well to an owner who is born under the sun sign of Taurus. There is also a chance of a good relationship with a Cancer or Sagittarian owner – if the human does not tend to be overly critical.

If you are an Aquarian or a child of Capricorn, you would be well advised not to acquire a cat born under the sign of Cancer. Likewise, if your sign is Libra, Scorpio, Gemini or Aries, you would be better off with a feline from some other zodiacal home.

Someone born under the sun sign of Pisces is the perfect owner for the Cancer cat, and it is in such a relationship that two-legged and four-legged will walk almost as one. If they were willing to make a commitment to work at it, Leos and Virgos could also have a chance of a harmonious relationship with the Cancer cat.

The Leo cat – 23 July to 23 August

If your thing is taking prizes in cat shows, you should make it a point to see that all your felines were born under the sign of Leo. Your Leo cat will love to be in the limelight; and should entering contests not appeal to you, you will have a little furry show-off at home.

Your Leo cat will exhibit a great deal of personal magnetism and will undoubtedly charm every member of your family.

Basically of robust health, the Leo cat may tend to injure the muscles of its back.

Adaptability is another of the Leo cat's most positive attributes, so it will fit comfortably into nearly any environment. If possible, you should see that it always has plenty of room in which to exercise. If your Leo cat could speak, it would probably express a preference for the mountains, rather than a swamp or a marsh, but it will provide you with excellent company wherever you choose to reside.

Since Leo cats are so adaptable, they will be compatible with most humans. Their relationships will probably be strongest with those born under the signs of Aries, Leo and Libra; less so with owners from the signs of Taurus, Scorpio, Capricorn and Sagittarius.

The potential owners whose signs are Gemini, Cancer, Virgo, Aquarius and Pisces will have to work a bit harder than some to make a solid union with the Leo cat, but the potential for harmony is definitely there.

The Virgo cat — 24 August to 22 September

Cats born under this sun sign tend to be somewhat aloof and standoffish. Those cat lovers who adore their pets for being so independent and self-contained should acquire only Virgo cats.

Although the Virgo cat is usually not very strong physically, paradoxically, they are very often quite long-lived.

In spite of their cool and aloof dispositions, they are extremely sensitive to discord. If there should be an argument in your family, you will quite likely have a cat with an upset stomach on your hands. Because of their tendency to digestive disorders, you will be advised to keep a careful check on your Virgo cat's diet.

Virgo cats fit in well on farms, wooded uplands and areas where there are meadows and grazing lands. Keep your Virgo feline away from places were there is excessive dampness or wet mists.

Taurean owners very often get along quite well with Virgo cats. There can also be great compatibility with humans born under the sun sign of Capricorn. Less likely positive relationships exist between Virgo cats and owners born under the signs of Aries, Cancer, Sagittarius and Aquarius, but the unions can be made to work if the owner is willing to exercise patience.

If you are a Piscean or a Scorpio, forget about acquiring a Virgo cat. You would be in for a bumpy ride that would almost be fated to terminate in a collision. If your sign is Gemini, Leo or Libra, don't acquire a Virgo cat unless you are also desirous of acquiring a nervous breakdown.

The Libra cat – 23 September to 23 October

If you have a comfortable bank account, go ahead and acquire a cat born under the sign of Libra. Librans love to be pampered and fussed over. They can make great show cats, because they are especially proud of their personal appearance.

At the same time, your precious, pampered Libra pet will tend to be a bit on the moody and temperamental side.

The Libra cat tends to suffer from kidney problems, and you may expect bladder weakness as the cat grows older. In spite of these health troubles – and others that are more difficult to diagnose – the Libra cat generally lives to a ripe old age.

A house on a hillside would be heaven for the cat born under the sign of Libra. It would also be happy near the seashore, but you would have to monitor its exploration of the cliffs and high rocky areas, for the Libra cat tends to be more attractive than it is graceful.

The Libra cat is unlikely to be able to adapt to an owner born under the sign of Aries or Capricorn. A compatible relationship can work between the Libra feline and humans from the signs of Leo, Taurus, Pisces, Gemini and Libra.

A definite red light should flash if you are about to acquire a Libra cat and you were born under the signs of Cancer, Scorpio, Virgo or Sagittarius.

About the only green light the Libra cat can spot a mile off is a relationship with someone from the sign of Aquarius.

The Scorpio cat – 24 October to 22 November

Once you are able to gain the confidence of a Scorpio cat, you will have a passionate defender and a loyal feline – a cat that is basically very resourceful. Be prepared, however, for a flare of temperament every now and again.

Scorpio cats can find it difficult to be kept in close quarters, and they are happier out-of-doors and moving about the countryside. At the same time, their somewhat boisterous nature tends to make them a bit accident-prone.

As an attentive owner, you will have to keep a watchful eye on your Scorpio cat, for it will often overdo and tax itself if you do not keep it under control. Should it become ill, its temperature is likely to soar. Female Scorpio cats require special attention – especially if you should wish to breed them.

Basically, the Scorpio cat is very strong, and it will soon overcome nearly any illness. Your Scorpio is also blessed with great reserves of energy.

Scorpio cats are able to tolerate marshy ground and humid climates, but they are not quite as contented in cold, dry area. Your Scorpio feline would be happy next to a large body of water or the large expanses of the flatlands, where it can have the opportunity to roam every now and then.

If you were born under the sun sign of Aries, you should most certainly think twice before acquiring a Scorpio cat. You will eventually rub each other the wrong way and the fur will fly.

Nor will the Scorpio cat be likely to be your cup of catnip if you are a Taurus, a Gemini or an Aquarius.

You will be able to get along fairly well with your Scorpio fireball if you were born under the sun signs of Cancer, Leo, Virgo, Libra, Capricorn or Scorpio. Those owners born under the signs of Sagittarius and Pisces will be most contented with their Scorpio feline.

The Sagittarius cat – 23 November to 21 December

Your Sagittarius cat will probably drive you up the wall throughout its kittenhood, for freedom and lack of restraint seem to be its bywords. With a seemingly endless supply of liveliness and fire, your Sagittarius cat may simply wear you out if you permit it to express the full range of its impulsive behaviour. If the two of you can survive the wild days of its youth, however, you will find that you have a good, solid friend in its maturity.

You will also discover that even though your Sagittarius cat has mellowed a great deal as it becomes older, it has retained its physical vigour and attractiveness.

The Sagittarius cat has very few health problems, but you will need to look out for accidents to its legs during its robust youth.

You can live nearly anywhere you please with your adaptable Sagittarius – just as long as you make an occasional change of scene to provide it with a bit of variety in its environment.

If you were born under the sun signs of Gemini or Virgo, you have the least chance of complete harmony with the Sagittarius cat.

Owners born under the signs of Aries, Leo, Libra or Aquarius will have the best opportunity for full compatibility.

Be prepared for a bit more of gamble if you are a Taurus, Cancer, Capricorn, Sagittarius or a Pisces and you wish to acquire a cat from the sun sign of Sagittarius.

The Capricorn cat – 22 December to 20 January

Your Capricorn kitty is likely to be somewhat on the moody side, and you will need to be especially kind and gentle to stay on its good side. Under the best of circumstances, don't expect your Capricorn feline to be very demonstrative in terms of displaying affection.

Interestingly, you will find that your Capricorn cat will be more responsive to any children or teenagers that you might have in your household than to any adult. You will also soon observe that it will very much enjoy listening to music and watching certain television programmes.

The Capricorn cat has a tendency to have rather poor health in its kittenhood, and you will have quite a time settling upon a proper diet for its sensitive stomach. It does become stronger as it grows older, however; but watch for rheumatism in the mature Capricorn cat.

Large cities do not appeal very much to the Capricorn kitty's moody nature, but it seems very much at home in rural areas. Capricorns make excellent farm cats and will do their utmost to keep the rodent population thinned and bearable. A dry atmosphere works better for the Capricorn cat than a humid or damp environment.

An owner who is born under the sun sigh of Taurus has the temperament to create a very happy union with a Capricorn cat. A Virgo owner could also make a great match for the Capricorn kitty.

There are some chances of a harmony between a Scorpio owner and a Capricorn cat, and a Pisces owner could also make the relationship work.

A Gemini owner would have to learn to develop great patience should a Capricorn be added to the household, and Capricorn humans should carefully consider the risk in acquiring Capricorn cats.

A definite red light should flash in warning if you were born under the sun signs of Aries, Leo, Aquarius, Sagittarius, Cancer or Libra. You would be almost certain to consider a Capricorn cat to be a disruptive force in your household – whether it was or not!

The Aquarius cat – 21 January to 19 February

The Aquarius cat is often moody, eccentric in behaviour,

but nearly always the quintessential model of feline independence. If you wish to keep this cat reasonably contented, take it along with you on car trips wherever possible, for frequent changes of scene are necessary for its equilibrium.

If you, the owner, are somewhat on the unconventional side yourself, you will probably get along famously with the Aquarius cat. If you are basically a mellow person who doesn't sweat the details or allow yourself to become unglued over minor irritations, you will most likely have a tranquil and laid-back Aquarian cat. However, if you are easily upset or tend to get rattled and uptight emotionally, you will quickly see your stressed-out Aquarian cat mimicking your behaviour.

Because of its tendency towards moodiness, the Aquarius cat flourishes best in an environment as free of mental and emotional tensions as possible. And since it is sensitive to human stress levels, the Aquarius cat is susceptible to digestive disorders.

The Aquarius cat likes to dwell where it is high and breezy. It will be uncomfortable near marshy country or where there is stagnant water.

Aries, Leo or Virgo owners could establish a comfortable relationship with an Aquarian cat provided they are willing to allow for the moodiness of the feline.

The Aquarius cat would take a long time adjusting to the lifestyle of a Taurean owner; and Cancer or Capricorn owners probably just wouldn't be able to make the grade.

Owners born under the signs of Gemini, Sagittarius or Pisces would eventually be able to establish a harmonious household with their Aquarius cat.

Your best luck with the Aquarius cat would be if you are an Aquarian or a Libran. If you happen to be a Scorpio, you would be better off seeking a feline companion from some other sign in the zodiac.

The Pisces cat – 20 February to 20 March
The Pisces cat is a very affectionate feline, usually blessed

with high intelligence, but it does not possess a great deal of stamina.

Perhaps a bit too sensitive, the Pisces cat is very susceptible to illness and is usually not very strong physically. If it should dwell in a home where there is an undue amount of domestic strife between shouting spouses, the Pisces cat will soon be on the road seeking out a quieter domicile. Likewise, if there should be a gang of noisy children in the household, the Pisces feline will make itself scarce in a very short time.

A serene environment would seem to be at the very top of the Pisces cat's requirements for happy living, and it will not thrive especially well in a large city. The Piscean cat will most appreciate a place where there is water and an opportunity to stroll into the deep silence of nature.

There can be a harmonious union between the Pisces cat and owners who were born under the sun signs of Taurus, Gemini, Pisces or Libra.

If an effort is made to work for harmony, a Leo or Scorpio owner could build a good relationship with a Pisces cat.

If you were born under the sign of Aries, Capricorn, Aquarius, Sagittarius or Virgo, you would be better off not acquiring a Pisces cat. There would probably be tears of regret on both your part and the cat's.

However, if you claim the sign of Cancer as your birthright, you could enjoy a relationship with a Pisces cat that would far exceed your expectations. In fact, if your feline is a female, you might breed her in the hope of gaining even more Pisces cats.

A VISIT FROM THE ULTIMATE
FELINE/FEMININE ARCHETYPE

Imagine this: in one moment of linear time, you are standing speaking with your elder son in your farm home in Iowa. Suddenly, you feel very strange. There is a slight sensation of queasiness – and the next moment your face is crunching painfully into harsh grains of sand as you fall headlong on to the floor of an arena in some faraway dimension of time and space.

That is what happened to me on the night that I met Sekhmet, the lionheaded goddess, the ultimate feline archetypal expression of femininity.

I lay dazed and stunned on my face, and all around me I could hear what sounded like multitudes of hostile voices shouting for my death.

My God! Had I been transported back in time? Was I a fallen gladiator hearing the crowds screaming for my victorious opponent to administer the death blow?

And I really felt beaten, as though I could not move a muscle in my defence.

Then I slowly became aware that there was another chorus of voices that seemed to be on my side. They were shouting at me to get up. 'You can do it,' they cheered. 'Put your legs under you. Breathe deeply. Live! Live!'

For the first time I was able to lift my head, and I saw what appeared to be an ancient arena for trial by combat. But in spite of the raucous catcalls for my death and the earnest shouts for my return to the fray, I could see no one.

Dimly, I was aware that a figure stood near my fallen body. As I looked up to see if I would encounter friend or foe, I beheld a form that was unmistakably that of a woman of ebony flesh, but whose face was that of a dark-visaged lioness.

She reached down, took my hand in hers, and began to lift me to my feet. When she opened her mouth to speak my name and command me to get up, violent bolts of electricity shook my entire being.

Then the arena was gone . . . the black lionheaded woman was gone . . . and I was on my way to the hospital.

While I was struggling for my life in some in-between universe, my son and my late wife had called an ambulance, fearing the worst after my sudden collapse.

I was released from the hospital the next day after a series of physical tests were all graded 'A-plus'. I knew all the examinations were unnecessary, but how could I explain to my doctor friends at the hospital that I had been taken to another dimension and saved from defeat in the arena by a black lionheaded goddess?

I knew that something very significant had occurred to me on the night of 2 December 1974 at approximately two a.m., but it took me a little while to determine exactly what – and, of course, I may never know the full meaning of the mystical experience.

I was barely home from the hospital when a close friend of mine called to say that he had had a terrible dream in which I had been severely beaten, then rescued by a large, dark figure.

A medium friend of mine in Chicago telephoned that evening to say that on the night of my out-of-body experience, she had a vision in which she had seen me taken aboard a UFO to pass a test for a 'higher plane initiation'.

A few days later, a group of friends in San Francisco called to say that on the night of 2 December the lionheaded entity of Sekhmet had appeared to them as they sat in a meditative reverie. Sekhmet had transmitted my name to them.

Sekhmet, the lionheaded goddess, was one of the most ancient of deities, who came into Egypt in a time unrecorded from a place that is unknown. She is known as 'Lady of the Place of the Beginning of Time' and 'One Who Was Before the Gods Were'.

A goddess of enormous power, Sekhmet defends against all forces of evil. Also known as Lady of the Flame, the solar disc depicted on her head in various Egyptian statues signifies her control of the Sun. As consort of her husband-brother Ptah, the creative process, Sekhmet is the one found most beautiful by Art itself.

Perhaps no other Egyptian deity was represented by so many statues, but Sekhmet was possessed of a dual nature. She was the goddess of both love and war, healing and pestilence, cursing and blessing. Magicians and priests who sought power knew that the greatest source of all lay in Sekhmet, but they were also aware that they must maintain a proper spiritual balance or they would provoke her ferocious wrath.

At that time, our family owned four cats: three large, smoky greys and one calico. I admired our cats' feline stateliness when they happened to affect a pose underneath the statue of the Egyptian god Bast that sat atop a bookcase, but I can say that I had no great obsession with Egypt or with any cat god or any lionheaded deities. The statue of Bast had been a gift from my students when I had taught in high school and bore only sentimental, not spiritual, significance.

The bizarre thing was that Sekhmet had seemed so real, and I pondered the mystery of whether I had journeyed to her world in a time-outside-of-time or whether she had temporarily manifested in my dimension of time and space to present me with some kind of teaching vision.

At that time I was in regular correspondence with Robert Masters and his dynamic wife, Jean Houston, who had established the Foundation for Mind Research in Pomona, New York. When I was rummaging through some research papers that Bob had sent me, I was startled to see that he had conducted a series of experiments in which he and a female subject had entered the archetypal symbol system of the Egyptian goddess Sekhmet and her 'world'.

As soon as possible, I travelled to the Foundation for Mind Research where I was able to speak with Bob Masters, Jean Houston and Michele Carrier, the subject in the Sekhmet experiments.

Masters explained about a phenomenon in ancient Egypt called *Hanu*, which means 'being seized by the god'. And Sekhmet, through a statue of the goddess which he kept in a room, was regularly reaching out and grabbing people in the best ancient Egyptian tradition.

Ms Carrier saw Sekhmet as a historical representation of the archetype of the feminine. 'Sekhmet exists within the collective unconscious,' she said. 'She comes from a primitive state in the evolution of consciousness, but the symbols that are there can evolve within the consciousness of someone today. They may be primitive symbols, but they're still active today.'

Jean Houston expressed her opinion that Sekhmet's world existed in the archetypal imagination. 'She is an avatar of the female warrior goddess. Sekhmet is an activating archetype in a particular Egyptian mode.

'I think that there is emerging in our time the rise of the feminine in the psyche. This energy is manifesting as the traditional goddesses who have contained a great deal of energy with regard to the activating anima, such as Isis or Sekhmet or Mary.'

And what of the in-between universe or dimension in which archetypes such as Sekhmet exist?

Ms Houston replied that she believed that we are in a symbiotic process with it and that it has an 'apartness' from us. 'Reality is very thick,' she said. 'It is immensely complex.'

Ms Houston went on to express her pleasure and agreement with an image that William James uses in pragmatism. 'We are like dogs and cats who inhabit our drawing rooms. You know, happy and thinking about the food and the nap and going bye-bye, but having no idea at all of the intricate and fascinating goings-on around the house or what's in the bookcases.

'I think that is *our* level of reality,' Ms Houston said. 'We have a very, very tiny notion of what is reality. We are cats and dogs in the library. We are a psycho-spiritual process of which our own coding has barely been tapped.'

According to Ms Houston, such images as Sekhmet and other figures that may be considered deities or holy personages by certain individuals are able to become a reality to those who experience their manifestation. 'And it isn't just a reality that dwells inside,' she said, 'it has an objective reality.'

Such an image as that of Sekhmet relates to older areas of the brain, and thus is more related to the autonomic system, she explained. 'An image may impart a wave form to the bioplasmic field around. That wave form spreads to other kinds of frequencies, which then begin to attract what is necessary or even *create* that which is necessary.

'So can thought become flesh or attract its own objective reality through the impartment of the wave fields? Yes!' Ms Houston responded in affirmation to her own question. 'And that will be a way to explain, in part, the appearance of Jesus or the Virgin Mary or Sekhmet. Any image that is held long enough and intensely enough tends to become incarnate – incorporated and corporeal in the symbolic environment.'

FIND YOUR CAT'S POWER ANIMAL IN THE NATIVE AMERICAN ZODIAC

When I was relating my extraordinary experience with the archetype of the goddess Sekhmet to my friend Sun Bear, the great Chippewa medicine priest, I pointed out how strange it seemed to me that I should have an encounter with an Egyptian entity. Anyone who knows me or my work is aware of my great attraction to American Indian medicine power. It would seem, therefore, that my vision might have been more likely to manifest itself saturated with Native American symbolism.

'But Brother Brad,' Sun Bear smiled. 'We are always saying that all is one. Now you must also believe it. You see, you are born under the sign of the Cougar, so it wouldn't be strange for an entity that would appear as a great cat to come to your rescue in the in-between universe.'

I was puzzled. Sun Bear knew that I had been adopted into the Wolf Clan of the Seneca nation by the Repositor of Seneca Wisdom, Twylah Nitsch. What did he mean by saying I was born under the sign of the cougar, the mountain lion, the puma?

'Yes,' he nodded. 'The wolf may be one of your totems, but the great cat is your Medicine Wheel symbol.'

That was when Sun Bear explained to me about the

Medicine Wheel cosmology that he had realized through his visions and had expressed with the assistance of his Medicine Helper, Wabun. The Great Mystery had revealed to him a Native American zodiac, complete with representative totem animals.

I am certain that there are many readers who resonate to the colourful and dynamic symbols of American Indian Medicine and who would like to know how to determine their cat's (and maybe their own) totem power animal. Simply find the birth date of your cat below and study the implications for a better relationship between you and your feline companion. Some people have given their cats stuffed animals representing their totem animal or placed drawings of their feline's totem animal above the pet's bed in order to increase its opportunity for better balance on the Earth Mother. Remember, to the native Americans, all life is one – and your cat is entitled to a power symbol just as much as you are.

The Red Hawk – March 19 to April 19

Those born under the Native American zodiacal sign of the Red Hawk are likely to be adventurous and assertive. They cherish a desire to be free, and those closest to them may sometimes consider them a bit headstrong.

The Beaver – April 20 to May 20

Those of the Beaver sign are generally blessed with good health. They cherish peace and security, and they are thought by all to be loyal and stable.

The Deer – May 21 to June 21

Clever and talented entities are found under the sign of the Deer. Your cat will exhibit a generally positive disposition and will sometimes appear to be a creature of perpetual motion.

The Brown Flicker – June 22 to July 21

Entities born under this sign have a strong nesting instinct and are usually deemed to be good parents who provide responsibly for their young. Brown Flicker beings love peace and quiet and seek to avoid serious conflicts.

The Sturgeon – July 22 to August 21

Sturgeon beings have a great ability to teach others. They may be considered a bit domineering, but they generally bring a positive approach to every problem.

The Bear – August 22 to September 22

Those entities born under this sign of the Native American zodiac are usually slow, cautious, quiet and careful. Your cat companion born under the sign of the Bear is probably a no-nonsense feline who seems to be able to detect insincerity in others.

The Raven – September 23 to October 22

Raven beings are sociable and energetic, full of nervous energy and fluctuating moods. They are generally very flexible and adapt well to new environments and circumstances.

The Snake – October 23 to November 21

Charismatic, but often difficult to comprehend, Snake entities often present a problem to those around them. Those beings born under the sign of the Snake may hide a deceptive nature behind their charming exterior.

The Elk – November 22 to December 21

Elk beings are competitive and athletic, but they are also patient and kind. Those entities born under the sign of the Elk enjoy a change of scene every now and then – and cherish a strong independent streak.

The Snow Goose – December 22 to January 20

If your cat companion was born under the sign of the Snow Goose, you have a feline who is content to be at your side and who generally shows little interest in any dramatic alterations of the daily routine. Far from sluggish, however, the sign of the Snow Goose indicates a being with great stamina.

The Otter — January 20 to February 18

Otter beings are often regarded as unpredictable and mercurial. If your cat was born under the sign of the Otter, you will have a feline companion who will generally be good-natured and a loyal friend.

The Cougar — February 19 to March 20

Cougar beings are very mystical in nature. You will probably experience some fascinating telepathic link-ups with your Cougar cat. Watch your tone of voice and your unspoken attitude, as well, for those born under this sign are very sensitive and easily hurt by disapproval or rejection.